CONTENTS

WHAT'S THE BEVERAGE JOURNAL? IV

A BRIEF HISTORY OF THE MARYLAND LIQUOR INDUSTRY VI

ORIGINAL MARYLAND DRINK RECIPES XIII

HOW TAVERNS & CLUBS WERE CHOSEN FOR THE GUIDE XV

HOW TO READ THIS BOOK XVI

YUPPIE APPEAL XVII

MUNCH FACTOR XVIII

COMFORT ZONE XIX

BUD QUOTIENT XX

THE ENTRIES

Allegany County 1.
Anne Arundel County 7.
Baltimore City 17.
Baltimore County 43.
Calvert County 47.
Cecil County 53.
Charles County 58.
Frederick County 64.
Garrett County 71.
Harford County 76.
Howard County 80.
Kent County 86.
Montgomery County 89.
Pr. George's County 93.
Queen Anne County 100.
St. Mary's County 102.
Washington County 105.
Wicomico County 108.
Worcester County 114.

INDEXES 121.

What's The Beverage Journal? And Who's Michael L. Spaur?

For 54 years the *Maryland Beverage Journal* has been read every month by the owners and managers of every Maryland tavern, nightclub, restaurant (if it serves liquor), and liquor store. As the state's only magazine devoted to the dispersing of information to alcohol beverage manufacturers, wholesalers and retailers, the Journal has been nicknamed "The Bible" by members of the Maryland liquor industry.

Each month, the *Maryland Beverage Journal* reports on the newest beverages, drinks and industry legislation to appear throughout the state. And each issue carries an in-depth profile of at least one of Maryland's best taverns or clubs.

The *Guide to Maryland Taverns, Clubs & Bars,* a natural extension to the *Maryland Beverage Journal* and written by the magazine's editor, takes the reader behind the scenes at 101 of the state's best on-premise destinations from the shores of Deep Creek Lake in far Western Maryland to the shores of the Atlantic Ocean in Ocean City.

Michael L. Spaur, author of the Guide, has been writing about bars and nightclubs for 11 years. A graduate of Murray State University in 1977, he began his nightlife writing career with the *Frederick News Post* where he served for five years as the daily newspaper's entertainment editor and restaurant critic.

After a brief stint at freelancing, when he wrote alcohol beverage features and columns for periodicals including the *Washingtonian, Baltimore Magazine,* and California's *All About Beer,* he signed on with the Mid-Atlantic Food Dealer's Association as the editor of their trade magazine, *Skirmisher*. And 18 months later, on February 1, 1990, he quit writing about groceries and began writing about liquor as the new editor of the *Maryland Beverage Journal.*

Many of the entries in this Guide are nightclubs and taverns which Mike has written about in depth in the *Beverage Journal*, while others were discoveries he made while on the road researching the material for this book.

A (Very) Brief History Of Beer, Wine & Liquor in Maryland

On the following pages is a quick run through the Maryland alcoholic beverage industry's last 54 years. All of the information was collected from the *Maryland Beverage Journal* archives.

• 1938 •

The newest beer to enter the Maryland market comes from Detroit. It's an obscure brew called Stroh.

• 1939 •

The Calvert Distilling Company of Baltimore announces the creation of its first premium whisky - Lord Calvert.

• 1940 •

At the Third Annual National Beer Wholesaler's Convention, the beer rated as "Best Newcomer" is the new brew from the Jos. Schlitz Brewing Co. called Old Milwaukee.

• 1941 •

The driest California champagne ever marketed commercially, Korbel Brut, arrives in Maryland.

• 1942 •

The highest priced wine served in Maryland dining rooms is Mumm's Cordon Rouge averaging $7.50 per bottle, while the average retail price for Inglenook burgundy is $1.15 per fifth.

• 1943 •

The two largest selling products of the Heublein Corporation are Smirnoff vodka and A-1 steak sauce.

• 1944 •

The first major shipment of a Mexican beer - Carta Blanca - arrives in Maryland.

• 1945 •

In their recent advertising campaign, 7-Up promises America that their soft drink will always be sold in bottles and "never in syrup form for fountain or dispenser use."

• 1946 •

The following creme liqueurs are available in Maryland: creme de ananas (pineapple), creme de celeri (celery), creme de rose (rose petals), creme de violette (violets), and creme de yvette (also violets).

• 1947 •

The Seagram "Ancient" gin bottle (knotty head) replaces the traditional smooth bottle.

• 1948 •

Maryland consumers get their first chance at a wine cooler. It's made by Manischewitz.

• 1949 •

Dry Sack sherries have received a new package. Starting March 1, each bottle will be contained within a distinctive cloth sack.

• 1950 •

National Bohemian Beer is now available in flat-top cans which can be stacked much higher than conventional cap-sealed cans.

• 1951 •

National Bohemian is packaged for the first time in quart bottles.

• 1952 •

The newest blended whiskey of Maryland liquor store shelves is an Ohio product called Three Bucks and a Little Doe.

• 1953 •

The newest brew in Maryland is touted as being "the hottest new product in the industry today." It's called Country Club Malt Liquor.

• 1954 •

The beers of Jos. Schlitz Brewing Co. are the first to be packaged in 16-ounce cans.

• 1955 •

Miller High Life celebrates its 100th anniversary.

• 1956 •

Beginning March 1, all beer distributors must provide a minimum wage of $1 per hour to all employees.

• 1957 •

The newest imported beer to hit Maryland is Holland's Amstel (not the light version on the shelves today).

• 1958 •

A 40-acre site in suburban Halethorpe has been purchased by the Carling Brewing Company for their new Maryland brewery.

• 1959 •

Maker's Mark is the newest bourbon in Maryland. The bottle doesn't have the melted wax-covered neck, but does come with a hand-torn label.

• 1960 •

Richard's Wild Irish Rose wine comes to Maryland.

• 1961 •

For the first time since the beginning of Prohibition (1908), the sale of liquor by the drink is allowed in Harford County.

• 1962 •

The largest selling wine in Maryland is Thunderbird, which sells from 50 cents for a pint to $1.94 for a half gallon.

• 1963 •

The Carling Brewing Company test markets the "Tab Open" can in Baltimore to see if it receives any acceptance.

• 1964 •

Hennessy Cognac celebrates its 200th anniversary.

• 1965 •

The following gestures have been

More
Rock,
Than
Light.
ROCK
LIGHT

deemed unacceptable in beer and wine advertising: the tilting of a beer bottle; the holding of a bottle close to the lips; the wiping, smacking or pursing of lips; the swallowing motion of the Adam's Apple.

• 1966 •

Burnett's White Satin Gin, produced in Maryland, debuts in its home state.

• 1967 •

Maryland Governor Spiro Agnew tells the Maryland Board of Liquor License Commissioners that he wants tavern owners who have pinball machine on their premises to have their license revoked.

• 1968 •

Black Velvet, the fastest growing whiskey in Canada, is introduced to Maryland.

• 1969 •

Chocolate Driver comes to Maryland. Its a mix of white wine and imported Dutch chocolate. On the back label, it's suggested that the wine be served straight or poured over cake.

• 1970 •

Advertisements for Maryland's newest wine proclaim it to be "The Wine of the Century." The wine is M.D. Double 20 from Mogen David.

• 1971 •

Frost 8/80, the world's first clear whiskey, enters Maryland backed by a $2 million ad campaign. According to promoters, the new whiskey is a clearly better substitute for vodka and gin in mixed drinks.

• 1972 •

Exactly 12 months after the introduction of Frost 8/80, the brand is discontinued.

• 1973 •

Anheuser-Busch announces plans to build a $30 million Busch Gardens family entertainment complex in Williamsburg, VA.

• 1974 •

For the 27th year in a row, Seagram's Seven Crown is the largest selling brand of liquor in the country.

• 1975 •

Blue Nun wine has taken off in Maryland. Sales are up 800 percent over the previous year.

• 1976 •

For the first time in half a decade, Ruffino chianti comes out in a plain bottle instead of its traditional raffia (straw) wrapped squat bottle. It marks the end of an era of cheap candle holders.

• 1977 •

Touted as "the most exciting packaging job since sliced bread," Summit Premium wines are the first wines-in-a-box.

• 1978 •

Grolsch, the beer with a ceramic stopper, arrives in Maryland.

• 1979 •

Marylanders get their first taste of an Irish Cream liqueur. It's the one from Baileys.

• 1980 •

Absolut vodka comes to Maryland.

• 1981 •

Due in part to the success of the movie, "Urban Cowboy," the newest entertainment in Maryland suburban and rural taverns is the mechanical bucking bull.

• 1982 •

The newest Anheuser-Busch brew, Bud Light, arrives in Maryland.

• 1983 •

Country Western star Merle Haggard buys a single round of 5,095 Canadian Clubs & water at Billy Bob's Texas Bar in Fort Worth and makes it into the Guinness Book of World Records.

• 1984 •

Popov and Relska vodkas are the first spirits to be packaged in plastic bottles.

• 1985 •

DeKuyper's Apple Barrel schnapps becomes the fastest selling spirit in history.

• 1986 •

DeKuyper's Peachtree schnapps is the first spirit to break the million-case mark in six months.

• 1987 •

What are the hottest selling drinks in Maryland bars? Sex on the Beach is tops, followed by the Fuzzy Navel and Eastern Shore Lemonade.

• 1988 •

Maryland gets its first light beer brewed at a microbrewery - Samuel Adams Lightship.

• 1989 •

The newest entry to hop on the megabuck imported vodka bandwagon comes from Denmark and calls itself Denaka.

• 1990 •

It's Maryland's most expensive bottle of beer (retailing for up to $30 a bottle in taverns). It's the new (to Maryland) 3-liter bottle of Belgium's Corsendonk.

• 1991 •

The newest Maryland ultralight alcohol beverage is something called Taos.

• 1992 •

The first consumer publication devoted to the most interesting watering holes in Maryland is released by the *Maryland Beverage Journal.* The new book is entitled *The Beverage Journal Guide to Maryland Taverns, Clubs and Bars.*

Original Maryland Drink Recipes

A.M.F. SHOOTER

.25 oz. Absolut Citron
.25 oz. Absolut Vodka
.25 oz. Peachtree
.25 oz. Chambord
.5 oz. Triple Sec
Dash Rose's Lime
Dash Grenadine

Shake all ingredients over ice and strain into a rocks glass.

From the **Midway Cafe** in Essex

CAFFE RAMONA

.25 oz. Amaretto
.25 oz. Kahlua
.25 oz. Frangelico
.25 oz. Baileys
6 oz. Hot Black Coffee

Into an eight-oz. glass coffee mug, add coffee then four liqueurs. Top with whipped cream dusted with nutmeg and topped with a cherry.

From the **New Park Circle** in Hagerstown

DAVE'S PEACHTREE TEA

1.5 oz. Peachtree
.5 oz. Sour Mix
10 oz. Iced Tea

Fill a 16-oz. glass with ice cubes, add all of the ingredients and shake

From **Joe Theismann's** in Dorsey.

THE HOLLYWOOD

1 oz. Southern Comfort
1 oz. Sloe Gin
1 oz. Amaretto
Dash Orange Juice
Dash Pineapple Juice
Dash Milk

Shake together all ingredients over ice and strain into a rocks glass or serve over ice.

From the **Hollywood Show Bar** in Fells Point

BRAZEN BANANA

1 Ripe Banana
1 oz. Bacardi Light
1.5 oz. Creme de Banana
1 cup Ice

Put all ingredients into a blender and blend for 90 seconds. Pour into a large snifter. Garnish with banana slice.

From **Danny Nolan's** in Elkridge

DANGEROUS CURVES AHEAD

1 oz. Key Largo
.5 oz. Crown Royal
.5 oz. Captain Morgan
2 oz. Orange Juice

Shake all ingredients together and serve either on the rocks or straight up as a shooter.

From **Sierra Nite Club** in Hanover

HOT BUTTERED RUM

1 lb. Unsalted Butter
2 lbs. Lt. Brown Sugar
2 Whole Eggs
1 Tbsp. each:
Nutmeg
Cinnamon
Allspice
Light Rum
Hot Water

Blend the first six ingredients thoroughly and freeze. To make the drink, pour 1.5 oz. of light rum and one tablespoon of the frozen mixture into a coffee mug. Fill with very hot water and stir until completely blended.

From the **Swallow at the Hollow** in Baltimore

MT. WASHINGTON BLOODY MARY

1.5 oz. Vodka
8 oz. Tomato Juice
1 tsp. Horseradish
.5 oz. Beef Broth
2 dashes Worcestershire
1 dash Tabasco
Equal parts:
Salt
Pepper
Celery Salt

Shake together all ingredients over ice and pour into a 12-oz. highball glass. Garnish with a lemon wedge.

From the **Mt. Washington Tavern** in Baltimore

PEACHES IN A PEAR TREE

.5 oz. Peachtree
.5 oz. Pear Schnapps
.5 oz. Stolichnaya
Splash Soda Water

Shake together all ingredients over ice and strain into a shooter glass.

From **The Horse You Came In On** in Fells Point

BUTTERSCOTCH SUNDAE

1 oz. Butterscotch Schnapps
.5 oz. Amaretto
Dash Cherry Brandy
Scoop Vanilla Ice Cream

Thoroughly blend together all ingredients and serve in a soda shoppe glass.

From the **Holiday Inn Belmont** in Baltimore

GERMAN CHOCOLATE CAKE

.75 oz. Frangelico
.75 oz. Malibu
.5 oz. Chocolate Syrup
.75 oz. Half & Half
2 Scoops Vanilla Ice Cream
2 Scoops Crushed Ice

Place all ingredients into a blender and blend until smooth. Pour into a 12-oz. ice tea glass and garnish with whipped cream and shaved milk chocolate.

From the **Corner Bar** in Baltimore

CHERIE'S MARY

1 oz. Vodka
1 tbsp. Old Bay
1 tsp. Horseradish
1 tsp. Celery Seed
1 tsp. Lea & Perrin's
.5 tsp. Lemon Juice
.5 tsp. Lime Juice
6 oz. Tomato Juice

Rim a hurricane glass with Old Bay seasoning. Fill with ice. Add vodka, then other ingredients. Stir well and garnish with a celery stick.

From the **Patuxent Greens Country Club** in Laurel

SEX WITH A BARTENDER

1 oz. Grand Marnier
.75 oz. Chambord
1 oz. Cranberry Juice

Shake all ingredients over ice and strain into a rocks glass.

From **Regi's** in Federal Hill

KEY LARGO SWING

.5 oz. Key Largo Schnapps
.5 oz. Bacardi
.5 oz. Pineapple Juice
.5 oz. Orange Juice
.5 oz. Grenadine

Shake all ingredients over ice and strain into a rocks glass, or serve on the rocks in a highball glass.

From **Jerry's Belvedere Tavern** in Baltimore

CREAM SQUIRREL

1 oz. Kahlua
.5 oz. Baileys Cream
.5 oz. Frangelico
.5 oz. Vodka
2 oz. Half & Half

Shake all ingredients over ice and strain into a rocks glass.

From **101 Market Street** in Frederick

VANILLA BERRY

1.5 oz. Strawberry Liqueur
1.5 oz. Strawberry Schnapps
2 oz. Licor 43
3 oz. Pineapple Juice
3 oz. Orange Juice

Shake together ingredients and serve on the rocks in a highball glass. Garnish with a strawberry.

From **Phinian's Cafe** in Glen Burnie

BUTTERY RUSKI

(shooter version)

1 oz. Kahlua
1 oz. Butterscotch Schnapps
1 oz. Baileys Irish Cream

Carefully layer each of the liqueurs above (in the order given) into a rocks glass.

From **Phinian's Cafe** in Glen Burnie

Hey! How Come My Favorite Bar Isn't In This Book?

Chance's are that it isn't - mathematically speaking.

Throughout Maryland, there are just under 3,200 taverns, clubs and bars (and that's not including the hundreds of Maryland social, fraternal and military clubs). So, the chances of any one licensed establishment being included in this guide are about 32-to-1. Sure, we could have included all of them. But if we did, the guide wouldn't hit the shelves until 2008, and it would retail for around $250.00.

So, we decided to stick to highlighting 101 statewide watering holes.

What qualifications did we establish for admission to this guide? Basically, all of the entries included are taverns and clubs that contain a surprise, taverns and clubs that do things a little differently or offer the unexpected. These are not your run-of-the-mill gin joints.

Here are a few of the other things which the Guide entries aren't:

THEY ARE NOT MEGACLUBS

Do you really need to know more about places like *Hammerjacks*, *Studebakers* and *Baltimore's Original Sports Bar*?

THEY ARE NOT CHAIN TAVERNS

No cookie cutter taverns in this guide (Ok, just two). Although, by and large, the chain establishments are clean, comfortable and trendy, if you've seen one you've seen 'em all.

THEY ARE NOT HOTEL BARS

No modern hotel bars in here (OK, just one). Like chains, hotel establishments are exactly what you expect them to be.

THEY ARE NOT INNER HARBOR BARS

Nope, no Inner Harbor bars will be found here (OK, just one). The bars of the Inner Harbor are all great destinations. If they weren't, they wouldn't last long in Maryland's premier tourist hangout. If you want to know about the Inner Harbor spots, go to the Inner Harbor and take a walk. You don't need a guide to tell you about eight bars located on less than an acre.

What you will find in the Guide are great bars in towns like Clarysville, McHenry, Lusby and South Chesapeake City. You'll find bars that offer over 100 brands of beer or 200 wine labels or 300 different liquors. You'll find taverns that serve up hamburgers the size of duckpin bowling balls or shepherd's pie or pints of beer fresh from a brewery in the next room. You'll find a pub with 50 taps, and a bar filled with big game trophies.

If you can't find your favorite bar in the Guide, perhaps you'll discover one or two that are even better.

How To Read This Book

Congratulations! You've purchased the one and only book praising the accomplishments of Maryland tavern proprietors who go that extra mile for their patrons. Among these pages you'll find a tavern with 50 draft beers, a pub with 130 brands of bottled beer, a lounge with over 200 different wines, and a bar offering its patrons over 300 different liquors.

As you read the guide, you'll discover a beachfront hideaway surrounded by 30,000 square feet of tropical foliage, a small town tavern filled with big game trophy heads, and a suburban nightclub where the manager tosses 100 one dollar bills onto the crowded dance floor each week.

You'll read about Maryland's oldest bar, Maryland's biggest hamburger, Maryland's most coveted mai tai, and Maryland's only bar serving kangaroo sausage.

Entries in the Guide have been broken down by county beginning with Cumberland's Allegany and ending with Ocean City's Worcester. Each of the county sections is headed with a hand-drawn county map depicting the cities where the entries are located. WARNING: DO NOT USE THESE MAPS AS YOUR PRIMARY FORM OF NAVIGATION! These maps were not created by professional cartographers. About the only geographically-correct items on the county maps are those little doohickies that show where north is.

At the bottom of each write-up is a small box filled with the regular stats (hours, credit cards, etc.). The two lines of "Happy Hour" statistics, for the most part, just list the basics such as day and times. To see what the complete Happy Hour experience is at a particular spot, you're just going to have to pay the place a visit.

Under the heading of "Entertainment" in the bottom stat box, live entertainment will always take precedence. If no live acts appear at an establishment, the "Entertainment" lines will state the source of the background music (jukebox, stereo tapes & CDs, etc.)

On the following pages are explanations of the three scores and "Bud Quotient" found at the top of each entry.

Credit Cards: V=Visa MC=Master Card
AE=American Express D= Discover
DC= Diner's Club CB=Carte Blanche

There are about 3,200 taverns, clubs and bars in Maryland.
If you know of one that should be included in next year's guide, send it's name and description to:
THE GUIDE, 7451 RACE ROAD, P.O. BOX 1002, HANOVER, MD 21076-4002

Yuppie Appeal (0-5)

Unlike the other two scores (*Munch Factor & Comfort Zone*) ascertained by the author of the Guide, the *Yuppie Appeal* rating comes directly from the establishments' owners and managers.

Taverns with a "0" score in this category are much more likely to have a parking lot filled with Harley's and Ram Chargers rather than Beemers and Baby Benzs.

On the other hand, taverns with a "5" are likely to be filled (especially during Happy Hour) with power tie clad, Gold Card toting patrons sipping Absolut Bloody Mary's and discussing the merits of their new car fax machine.

Surprisingly, yuppie-intensive bars are not necessarily expensive watering holes. Owners of these establishments are well aware that a conspicuous-consumption lifestyle digs deeply into a yuppie's disposable cash, so drinks at yuppie bars can be very price-sensitive instead of pricey.

Yuppies also seem to be fond of themed taverns like the ones listed below:

ATMOSPHERES

ESTABLISHMENT	DECOR
Baltimore Brewing Co.	Boutique brewery
P.J. Crickett's	Turn-of-the-century luxury saloon
Donnelly's	1890's urban western saloon
Kitty Knight House	Jamestown tavern circa 1700
Last Chance Saloon	Modern English pub
Market Street Inn	Waterfront shanty
McGarvey's	Traditional American saloon
Milton Inn	Country manor circa 1790
Owl Bar	Turn-of-the-century luxury hotel bar
Ram's Head Inn	Rural British pub
O.C. Seacrets	Montego bayside watering hole
Stray Cat	Tijuana tourist bar
Tiki Bar	Florida Keys gazebo bar
Weber's on Boston	1920's speakeasy

Munch Factor (0-5)

The *Munch Factor* rating is not a subjective look at the foods offered in the various establishments featured herein, but rather an objective look at the variety of pub grub offered.

At the Milton Inn, for example, the cuisine is recognized as some of the best in the East, but it gets low scores in the Guide. Why? Although the Milton Inn's complete menu is available to tavern patrons, none of the offerings qualify as pub grub.

Pub grub is food that can be comfortably consumed barside. It's food that can be easily negotiated with one hand (burgers, sandwiches, pizza, onion rings, etc.) or appetizers served with one piece of silverware (chowder, potato skins, chili, etc.).

Taverns and such with high *Munch Factor* scores are those that offer great selections of **made-from-scratch** pub grub, and those that offer wonderfully weird and imaginative barside cuisine (check out Kangaroo Katie's alligator strips or kangaroo sausage).

Listed below is a more subjective look at some of the state's best pub grub.

BEST BITES

	PUB GRUB	ESTABLISHMENT
1.	Gourmet Pizza	La Trattoria
2.	Jerked Chicken	O.C. Seacrets
3.	Bacon Cheeseburger	Last Chance Saloon
4.	Un-Gourmet Pizza	Alonso's
5.	Shrimp & Andouille Gumbo	Sisson's
6.	Fried Clams	Kisling's
7.	Spicy Burrito	Cafe Tattoo
8.	Barbecued Brisket Sandwich	Scampy's II Afterdeck
9.	Crab Cake	Coins Pub
10.	Baked Brie w/Walnuts	Hummer's
11.	Shrimp Cocktail	J.B.'s Steak Cellar
12.	Smoked Bluefish Appetizer	Pirate's Cove
13.	Cheeseburger	Naughty Gull
14.	Homemade Cheese Sticks (free)	Schaefer's Canal House

Comfort Zone (0-5)

Of the three ratings on each of the entries, *Comfort Zone,* was the hardest to quantify. Some of the best destinations in the Guide have a rating of 5 in this category. And some of the best destinations in the Guide have a 0 or 1.

Two entries which lie on opposite sides of the *Comfort Zone* spectrum are Andy's and The Cat's Eye Pub. Andy's rates a "5" on the comfort scale. It's lounge is filled with couches and wing-back chairs, and once settled in, it's hard to leave. The Cat's Eye Pub gets a goose egg for comfort. On weekend nights, the place is packed tight with a SRO audiences. Even finding a place to set your beer is a challenge. But standing for an entire evening at the Cat's Eye is a "shared experience" among the patrons which adds to the charm of the place.

Listed below is some of the prime real estate in Maryland taverns - the seats which patrons hate to relinquish once they've been secured.

BEST SEATS IN THE HOUSE

Listed below are some of the most comfortable, most scenic or most coveted tavern seats in Maryland - the ones which are claimed early and not given up without a fight

	TAVERN	SEAT - LOCATION
1.	Andy's	Any chair or sofa in the lounge
2.	Donnelly's	Second-story window seats
3.	Silver Tree	Fireside sofa (winter)
4.	Griffin's	The banquette in front of the hearth (winter)
5.	Dead Eye's Saloon	The sofa on the deck (summer)
6.	La Trattoria	East Street-side window seats
7.	Rusty Scupper	South balcony deck chairs (summer)
8.	Johnny & Sammy's	Sectional sofa surrounding hearth (winter)
9.	Schaefer's	Window seats along the C&D Canal
10.	Tell Tale Hearth	Window seats facing the Hollins Market
11.	Henny's	Fireside booths (winter)
12.	Cat's Eye Pub	Any bar stool (weekend evenings)
13.	Sisson's	Same as above

Bud Quotient ($1.40 - $4.50)

During the planning stages for the *Guide to Maryland Taverns, Clubs & Bars,* we decided not to label the establishments with the typical cost ratings (expensive, moderate, etc.). Instead, we opted to choose a beverage which we thought was common to every on-premise operation in the state - Budweiser, the king of beers.

It wasn't until we started our research that we discovered that the "king" is dead in at least three taverns.

The *Bud Factor* is the normal price of a 12-ounce Budweiser (not a deflated Happy Hour price or inflated band price).

Although Bud is still Maryland's best-selling brew, there are over 175 beers and ales available to the Marylanders, and one of the joys of tavern-hopping should be the discovery of something new.

Is your favorite beverage found in the left hand best sellers list below? If it is, try one of the picks listed at right the next time you visit a tavern. You might just be pleasantly surprised!

ALTERNATIVES

IF YOU DRINK:	YOU SHOULD TRY:	OR, (IF YOU CAN FIND IT):
Budweiser	Steinlager	Golden Eagle
Coors Light	Amstel Light	Kirin Light
Bass	Whitbread	Old Peculier
Sharp's	St. Pauli Girl N/A	Haake-Beck
Jim Beam	Maker's Mark	Blanton's
Seagram's Gin	Beefeater	Bombay Sapphire
Bacardi	Mt. Gay	Cockspur
DeKuyper Peppermint	Goldwasser	Rumple Minze
DeKuyper Peachtree	n/a	Pecher Mignon
Dewars	Chivas Regal	Pinch 15 yr.
Glenlivet	Oban	The Macallan
Jose Cuervo	Jose Cuervo 1800	Hussong's
Absolut	Wyborowa	Ketel One

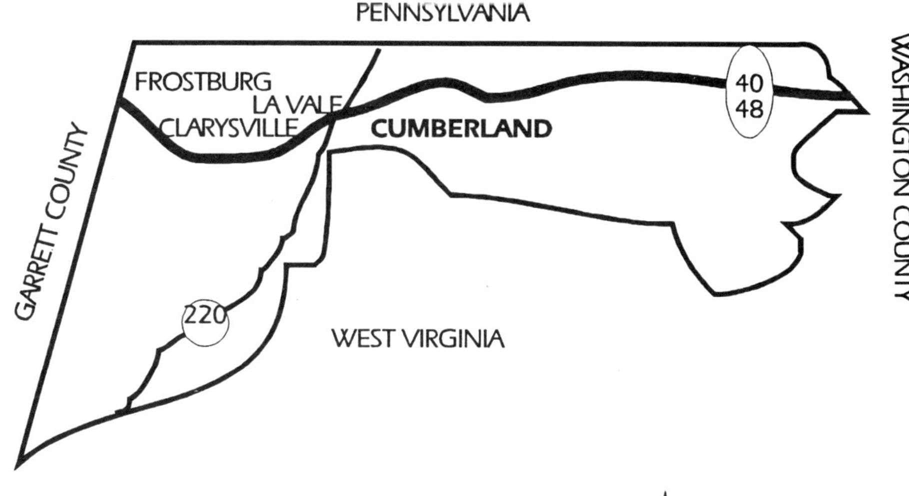

Area: 426 sq. miles
Population: 72,700

GLADSTONE'S

11 W. Main Street
Frostburg, MD
(301) 689-6511

YUPPIE APPEAL 4
MUNCH FACTOR 3
COMFORT ZONE 2
BUD QUOTIENT $1.50

Gladstone's is like a beautiful woman who doesn't know how beautiful she really is. The only adornments in the bar inside the 96-year-old Failingers Hotel in downtown Frostburg are the massive gold chandeliers hanging from the 20-foot high ceiling. The bar (as well as the entire hotel) went through an extensive restoration six years ago, and today it looks much the way it must have back in the late nineteenth century.

Instead of being the staid and proper watering hole one would expect such an establishment to be, Gladstone's is the sight of Buffalo wing (10 cents apiece) feeding frenzies on Wednesday evenings (2,500 of those fowl appendages pass over the bar on a good night). It's the only tavern in town that thought of serving a "Peewee Herman" (Jack & Squirt). And it's the site of 35-cent drafts. Gladstones may have all of the trappings of a grand ballroom, but it serves as a watering hole for Frostburg State students - so allowances will be made.

Aside from the dime wings, evening specials inside Gladstones include mini-burgers (three for a buck), 75-cent foot longs, slabs of fresh dough pizza for 35 cents, and Tex-Mex cuisine starting for a quarter (Frostburg students aren't known for their disposable cash reserves).

A couple of domestic drafts and around 20 bottled brews are the big sellers there, followed by mixed drinks in the shooter or frozen mode, and one night a week (Tuesday) everything at the bar is two-for-one.

Gladstones tavern menu boast such goodies as half-pound burgers *stuffed* with a varieties of cheeses, meats and veggies served between thick slices of homemade French breads, 14 varieties of salad featuring house cured and smoked meats, and most every entry comes with a pile of homemade potato chips.

After the recent renovation, the current hotel owners found enough artifacts to fill a museum - so they built a museum. Beneath Gladstones is a small labyrinth filled with displays of turn-of-the-century bottles, books and clothing, plus a fully restored jail cell and cock-fighting arena used by the hotel's first owner.

HOURS: Mon. 5-2; Tues.-Sat. 11-2; Sun. 1-5

HAPPY HOUR: Mon.-Sat. 3-5, discount munchies and 35-cent drafts

ENTERTAINMENT: Tues.-Sun. 1-2 piece live acoustic

ACCEPTABLE PLASTIC: V, MC, AE

BEST TIME TO VISIT

Gladstones peaks on Saturday nights during the school year.

HENNY'S

1268 National Highway
La Vale, MD
(301) 729-3300

YUPPIE APPEAL 4
MUNCH FACTOR 3
COMFORT ZONE 3
BUD QUOTIENT $1.90

You'd expect to find a place like this tucked inside an Inner Harbor Pavilion, along the Annapolis waterfront, or in old town Ellicott City. The only things Western Maryland about the place are the prices. Carved into the northern half of LaVale's Gehauf's restaurant is a two-story room filled with plants, pine, brass and director's chairs called Henny's.

Patrons there have the option of relaxing in large comfortable booths across from the bar, sitting on the upper level lounge across from a a roaring fire, retiring to the loft above the main lounge to just kick back and listen to the blues CD discs, or watching the world go by from the outdoor deck during the spring and summer.

Boasting the biggest brew selection in the Cumberland metro area, Henny's serves 22 different flavors including many unheard of labels in the other area bars: Anchor Steam, Kirin, Dos Equis Special Lager, pints of Grolsch, etc. But the selection process doesn't stop there.

Eleven varieties of wine are offered in single servings (including an Asti spumante), and Henny's has one of the largest wine lists in the region containing some of California's and Europe's better vintages at a price Baltimoreans wouldn't believe.

Instead of grabbing their wine coolers from a four-pack, Henny's bartenders make theirs up fresh to order, and mixes are never incorporated into their large selection of coladas (including a "Very Berry Pink Ice made with a combination of five berries) and daiquiris. For those who prefer their potables a bit more potent, Henny's has its own "Heavy Hitters" drink category where the most expensive ($3.50) drinks reside (Zombies, et al).

From the kitchen comes a tavern menu as complete as the beverage inventory. All of the fresh fried finger foods are there (fried cheese, original-recipe wings, beer battered onion rings) along with a dozen sandwiches, six salads and a couple soups du jour costing between 95 cents and $1.50 for a seafood chowder or bisque.

BEST TIME TO VISIT

The best crowd at Henny's arrives at Henny's by 6 p.m. on Thursdays and Fridays.

HOURS: Mon. -Thurs. 4:30-12; Fri.-Sat. 4:30-1; closed Sun.

HAPPY HOUR: None

ENTERTAINMENT: Blues & easy listening via CD stereo

ACCEPTABLE PLASTIC: V, MC, AE

ALLEGANY COUNTY

J.B.'S STEAK CELLAR

Exit 46, Interstate 68
Cumberland, MD
(301) 722-6155

YUPPIE APPEAL	4
MUNCH FACTOR	4
COMFORT ZONE	4
BUD QUOTIENT	$1.75

When I lived in Cumberland seven years ago, there was no industry. There were no jobs, and the major currency was the Food Stamp. But change was in the air. The highway linking Cumberland with urban Maryland was being widened; a new federal prison was coming to Allegany County; and major industries were, once again, taking a serious look at Cumberland.

By 1989, the economic upswing in Western Maryland was creating new niches in the food & beverage industry. It was time to go upscale.

For the past three years, J.B.'s Steak Cellar has been tapping Cumberland's newly gained wealth. J.B.'s has, among other things, cleverly transformed prime rib from a traditional once-a-year-special-occasion entree to an impulse item.

You'll enter into a small, well-lit dining room which features a glass-enclosed butcher's case displaying the various cuts available on the menu. And the centerpiece of that display is an entire rib section ready to be carved and cooked to order (it's butter-tender prime rib).

Leaving the main dining room, you'll enter a small square lounge with a large stone fireplace at one end, a dark hardwood bar, boasting a grand mahogany and stained glass backbar, at the other end, and large comfortable booths running along the sides. The music flowing through the lounge is the soft jazz of the 20s and 30s, and the waitstaff is clad in subdued Roaring Twenty's attire. Carrying that subtle "Speakeasy" theme, J.B.'s lounge has made its mark in Cumberland by appealing to the older (35 & up) white collar patron.

The majority of the two dozen beers offered at J.B.'s are the imported and upscale domestic variety (a dark brew and rare beef is a wonderful match), and an extensive wine list features top wines (Mondavi, Mirassou, etc.) by the glass, all priced below $3 a serving.

The entire menu is available both in the lounge and at the bar with the best bites being a slab of that rib, or a $5.95 shrimp cocktail containing five 12-count beauties that are a meal in themselves.

HOURS: Mon.-Thurs. 7 a.m.-11; Fri.-Sat. 7 a.m.-12

HAPPY HOUR: None

ENTERTAINMENT: Jazz of the 1930s and 1940s via CD stereo

ACCEPTABLE PLASTIC: All but CB

BEST TIME TO VISIT

Both the bar stools and booths in J.B.'s Steak Cellar fill on weekend evenings. Call early in the day and reserve yourself a booth.

SCAMPY'S II

Rte. 40 between La Vale & Frostburg
Clarysville, MD
(301) 689-3900

YUPPIE APPEAL 3
MUNCH FACTOR 3
COMFORT ZONE 4
BUD QUOTIENT $1.75

Between LaVale and Frostburg along the old National Highway is a small rural hamlet called Clarysville. How small? The entire community fit comfortably inside Scampy's II, the largest Maryland nightclub west of Hammerjacks.

From the front of the structure housing Scampy's II, it's impossible to guess what's contained inside. There's a seafood restaurant (Scampy's) in the front of the huge white Georgian manor, but in the back half there's a huge DJ-driven nightclub. The best surprise, though, lies beyond the club.

It's called Scampy's II Afterdeck; a three-level deck, half covered, half open. About 10 different beers are offered from the huge Afterdeck bar, and wine sales are all but non-existent. But if your tastes lean toward the frozen side of the spectrum, this is your kinda place. Over 100 blended drinks such as the "Nutty Monkey" and "Razzmatazz" are created on the Afterdeck.

To set itself apart from the competition (as if size and location were not enough), the owners of Scampy's II motored down to Texas and brought back a 4,500-pound meat smoker. Utilizing 100 percent hickory for fuel, the smoker creates mouth-watering ribs plus brisket entrees and sandwiches. And sizzling on an outdoor grill are the usual fare (chicken, pit beef and tenderloins) plus fresh tuna and swordfish steaks.

Each summer Friday between mid-June and the end of July, the Scampy's II Afterdeck serves as the venue for the regional Miss Hawaiian Tropic Pageant. The weekly event draws an average audience numbering over 300.

During the weekends, the Afterdeck is one of Western Maryland's hottest destinations, but during the week, patrons can sit back with a frozen something and quietly take in the surrounding scenery.

Gregarious types should head to the Afterdeck on the first Saturday after July 4th for Scampy's "Summer Jam '92," replete with five bands, beer trucks and dancing in the parking lot until two.

BEST TIME TO VISIT

The frozen drink machines and grills are running at full capacity on summer Saturdays. Get there before 8 for a good deck chair.

HOURS: Wed.-Sun. 5-2, closed Mon.-Tues.

HAPPY HOUR: Fri. 5-7 large free buffet featuring either crab or shrimp

ENTERTAINMENT: Wed.-Sun. DJ rock inside or live music on deck

ACCEPTABLE PLASTIC: V, MC, AE

THE WINE CELLAR

Exit 46, Interstate 68
Cumberland, MD
(301) 777-3553

Take a seat at the bar in the Wine Cellar, then take a look around. That stonework around the backbar was laid by Col. William Lamar in 1790. Those huge chestnut beams above your head are also two centuries old. The cellar in the Georgian mansion that houses the L'Osteria Restaurant may never have been used to store wine, but it's one of the oldest (if not **the** oldest) tavern settings in Maryland.

Heat in the bar is provided by a small Franklin stove and, in the adjacent lounge, by a large glassfront wood stove. It's the place to be on a cold winter's eve.

A dozen imports (mostly darks) head the beer list at the Wine Cellar.

HOURS: Mon.-Sat. 4-12; closed Sun.

HAPPY HOUR: Fri.-Sat. 4-7 discount drinks

ENTERTAINMENT: Soft rock & contemporary music via stereo

ACCEPTABLE PLASTIC: V, MC. AE

YUPPIE APPEAL	4
MUNCH FACTOR	3
COMFORT ZONE	3
BUD QUOTIENT	$1.75

Seven still wines and a sparkler come in single servings, and the massive oak backbar supports a full complement of spirits including some entries you've never seen before: Italian aperitifs and liqueurs brought in by the owner from vacation trips.

Although the Frostburg Jazz Quintet drops by the Cellar on occasion to play for drinks, entertainment is limited to soft rock and country stereo - except twice a year, when the boys from P.G. County's Hangar Club (featured herein) come to town. No men are allowed entry when the Hangar's Male Revue is in progress.

The Wine Cellar menu is filled with both traditional and rare offerings. Gucci (designer) potato skins are custom-made by the patron from a list of seven ingredients, and their french fries are created from homegrown spuds and doused with homemade cheese sauce.

Gourmet pizzas there can come topped with steak or artichoke hearts or prosciutto. And pasta is served up in all the shapes from lasagna to penne.

Your bartender will probably be Oz Gigliotti, the owner of the place, and he'll want to tell you about the cannon ball lodged in the Revolutionary War-era structure's frame. He'll tell you how the house served as a Civil War hospital, and he'll tell you about the ghost, whom the locals refer to as "The Colonel."

Here's another historical tidbit. The marble slabs topping the bar in the Wine Cellar once served as urinal partitions in the old Annapolis Court of Appeals. I guess you *really* didn't have to know that.

BEST TIME TO VISIT
Any cold winter's night.

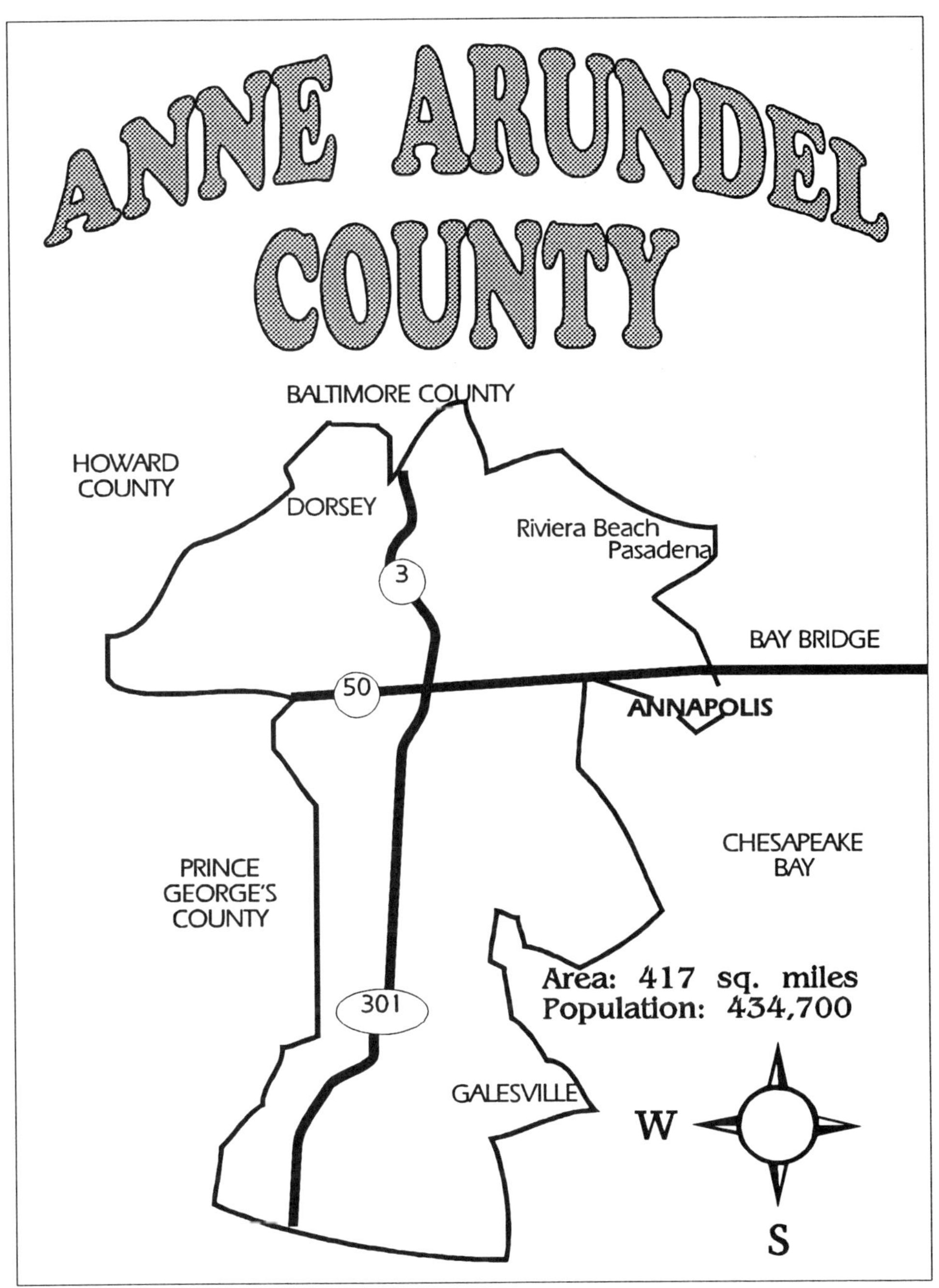
ANNE ARUNDEL
COUNTY
BALTIMORE COUNTY
HOWARD
COUNTY
DORSEY
Riviera Beach
Pasadena
3
BAY BRIDGE
50
ANNAPOLIS
CHESAPEAKE
BAY
PRINCE
GEORGE'S
COUNTY
Area: 417 sq. miles
Population: 434,700
301
GALESVILLE
W
S

A.L. GATOR'S

8501 Fort Smallwood Road
Riviera Beach, MD
(410) 255-2132 (info) 255-5533

There's more happening in one third of A.L. Gators than in any other Anne Arundel nightclub. It's a dance bar, a party bar and a sports bar all under one roof.

The Gators "Wreck Room," which appears to have been decorated by Sanford & Son, has all manner of junk hanging from the walls. Tables are overturned galvanized wash basins. Chairs are car seats salvaged from auto graveyards. And in one corner there sets a 1960 VW Microbus. Four separate bars are situated throughout the Wreck Room, with one solely responsible for dispensing frozen drinks (16 different varieties) and imported beer (over 30 different brands).

HOURS: Thurs., Sat.-Sun 8:30 p.m.-2; Tues. 5-2; Fri. 4:30-2

HAPPY HOUR: Fri. & Tues. 5-8:30 half-price drinks

ENTERTAINMENT: Thurs.-Sat. live progressive/R&B

ACCEPTABLE PLASTIC: V, MC. AE

YUPPIE APPEAL 4
MUNCH FACTOR 1
COMFORT ZONE 3
BUD QUOTIENT $2.50

Live music plays nightly in the Wreck Room.

The Gators "Dance Room" is ruled by Brian "Mad Dog" Brian, the house DJ who spins a mix of rock & schlock, and host a variety of nightly competitions such as "Eat the Weinie," and "Suck it Dry" (use your imagination). The centerpiece of the dance room is a huge octagonal bar with a raised dance floor in the center.

The Gators "Sports Bar" on the upper level boasts foosball and pool tables, air hockey, pinball machines and an indoor volleyball court complete with sand.

Throughout all three room inside the complex are tubs filled with bottled beer for sale, each manned (womanned) by a bikini-clad vendor.

If all of this isn't enough, even the weekly promotions at A.L. Gators are unlike any other in Maryland (I swear I'm not making the last two up). On Tuesdays, draft beer goes for 75 cents all night. On Thursdays, ladies pay $6 and drink all they want and anything they want all night. On Fridays (here's where things start to get a little weird) they do something called the "Gator Buck Drop." Near closing hour, the manager throws 100 one dollar bills from the second floor balcony to the dance floor below. And Sunday is "Loco Motion" night, when all mixed drinks are a buck, and ladies drink anything they want for free until 10 p.m.

Food at A.L. Gators is slabs of pizza, soft pretzels and hot dogs, plus raw bar cuisine in the Wreck Room.

BEST TIME TO VISIT

Ladies should get there on Sundays at 8:30...so should men.

GRIFFIN'S

20-22 Market Space
Annapolis, MD
(410) 268-2576

YUPPIE APPEAL	5
MUNCH FACTOR	4
COMFORT ZONE	4
BUD QUOTIENT	$2.75

I asked the proprietor of Griffins what he thought the *Yuppie Appeal* of his establishment should be. He said "Four." No way. It's a "five." As soon as you walk into the bar, you'll see that this is no ordinary tavern, even by the high standards set by downtown Annapolis watering holes. Look at the huge 25-seat mahogany bar top with pink marble. Look at the backbar supported by massive hardwood pillars. Look up and see the stamped tin above the bare brick walls, and the ceiling which rises 35 feet above the center of the lounge space. The seats are upholstered banquettes, and there's enough brass and foliage to satisfy the most demanding Baby Benz owner.

OK, Fine. The place has all of the yuppie trappings, but is the theme carried at the bar? But, of course. The specialty de la tavern is something called Cappuccino L'Amour, a $4.50 concoction made of the title beverage and 12 liquors and liqueurs including Galliano, brandy and creme de cocoa. That's just one of over a dozen super specialty sweet drinks offered at Griffins' bar. Utilizing a host of cordials, including 17 super-premiums, bartenders there construct a large variety of frozen jobs like Blue Cuervo margaritas, and Frozen Nuts & Berries, plus spiked offerings made with espresso, coffee and hot apple cider.

There are eight different wine varieties (four white - four red) served up by the glass. The majority of the bottled beers are the import and microbrew variety including Philly's Dock Street Amber and Beck's Pint Bombers. And draft beers, including Sam Adams and Molson Light, can be ordered in 23-oz mugs for $4.95. But those beer prices take a real nosedive during happy hour, when domestic keg beer can be had for under a buck.

Griffins' grub matches its potent potables. Their hot crab dip served with a loaf of freshly-baked bread in the most popular bar treat, but they also have potato skins immersed with cheddar and bacon, big burgers topped with goodies like jalapenos and Monteray jack or fresh mushrooms and melted smoked gouda, and a Southwestern Chicken sandwich covered in melted jack, diced tomato and green chilis.

BEST TIME TO VISIT
Friday happy hour.

HOURS: Mon.-Sun. 11-2

HAPPY HOUR: Mon.-Fri. 4-6:30 discont beer & food specials

ENTERTAINMENT: Eclectic mix of tunes via CD stereo & tapes

ACCEPTABLE PLASTIC: All but D

McGARVEY'S SALOON

8 Market Space
Annapolis, MD
(410) 263-5700

Is this your idea of a night on the town: kicking back in a lounge chair watching *Americas Funniest Videos*, drinking a guava colada and munching on French bread slathered with goose liver? If so, I don't think you'll get a kick out of McGarvey's.

There's no TV. There are no "sissy blender drinks" (their phrase), and no nouvelle (la-di-dah) cuisine. You won't see McGarvey's patrons participating in wet t-shirt contests, or making fools of themselves via a karaoke machine. The tavern at the eastern end of Annapolis' Market Space refuses to be anything more than a traditional American Saloon.

HOURS: Mon.-Sat. 11:30-2; Sun. 10-2

HAPPY HOUR: Nov. 1 - April 15, Mon.-Fri. oyster bar discounts

ENTERTAINMENT: Mixed music via CD, tape and satellite

ACCEPTABLE PLASTIC: V, MC, AE

YUPPIE APPEAL	4
MUNCH FACTOR	4
COMFORT ZONE	3
BUD QUOTIENT	$2.85

Tiffany lamps illuminate the huge, dark birch bar in the main room at McGarvey's surrounded by brick walls and a 120 year-old stamped tin ceiling. Over 20 different brews are offered at that bar, including Aviator's Amber Lager made exclusively for McGarvey's by a Virginia microbrewery.

House wines are by Robert Mondavi vineyards and there's a special wine-by-the-glass menu which changes weekly. And an all-inclusive spirit selection fills the shelves on the enormous, custom-made mahogany backbar.

So, what does one eat in a traditional saloon? He eats two-fisted burgers, crabcakes and grilled chicken sandwiches most days of the week. But on Mondays, he opts for a fiery combination of New Orleans style red beans and rice. And on Fridays (and only Fridays) he orders a mountain of McGarvey's elaborate nachos stuffed with 12 different ingredients. Due to the time it takes to construct that dish, it's only offered Fridays evenings.

For those who feel compelled to consume seafood when they visit Annapolis, McGarvey's has it's own Oyster Bar room that's as big as its main barroom. Filled with plants and ceiling windows (plus its own sit-down bar), it's like eating in an arboretum.

With a kitchen open until 1 p.m. every night, McGarvey's is a good spot to finish up an evening at the Annapolis waterfront.

BEST TIME TO VISIT

Even standing room at McGarvey's is at a premium during the weekends. Try the place in the early evening during the week.

MIDDLETON'S TAVERN

2 Market Space
Annapolis, MD
(410) 263-3323

YUPPIE APPEAL 2
MUNCH FACTOR 3
COMFORT ZONE 3
BUD QUOTIENT $2.50

Throughout the downtown waterfront region of Annapolis, there are a dozen first class taverns. Any establishment less than first class just couldn't survive the region's rarefied nightlife atmosphere. If the test of time is any indicator of an Annapolis pub's prowess, the 140-year-old Middleton Tavern is the king of the harbor.

Originally owned and operated by Horatio Middleton (and later by his son, Samuel), the tavern served as a watering hole frequented by such notables as George Washington, Thomas Jefferson and Ben Franklin.

During the following decades, the place served as a general store and meat market, a soda shop, as well as a number of food and drink operations under a variety of names. But the present owners, who took over in 1968, restored the tavern's original title.

It's pretty much a non-yuppie crowd that occupies the first-floor pub/oyster bar at the Middleton Tavern. There, they can select from five different drafts (including a signature brew called Samuel Middleton's Ale), eight different wine offerings by the glass, and a complete liquor selection. They also come for the Middleton Oyster Shooter - a shot glass filled with a fresh shucked prime oyster doused with cocktail sauce and a glass of beer - all for 95 cents.

Every night, there's entertainment in the downstairs tavern provided by regional acoustic folk and rock musicians. And every Monday night, all tavern patrons are invited to the "Monster Lobster Extravaganza" where the customer who comes closest to guessing the lobster's weight wins it.

Upstairs at the Middleton Tavern, there's the Arundel Room, a warm and cozy area with it's own sit-down bar, a fireplace and a piano bar. Open only on weekend evenings, the Arundel Room is a nice change of pace from the traditional Annapolis night scene.

But the best seats in the house are not in the house. The Tavern's huge front porch is the perfect spot to sit back with a cold beer and watch the world (and the girls) go by.

BEST TIME TO VISIT

If you get there on a Tuesday evening, not only will you avoid the crowd, but you'll hear the Tavern's top group, *Van Dyke & Glaser*.

HOURS: Mon.-Fri. 11:30-1:30; Sat. 11-1:30; Sun. 10-1:30

HAPPY HOUR: None

ENTERTAINMENT: Mon.-Sun. 10-closing one- to four-piece acoustic bands

ACCEPTABLE PLASTIC: V, MC, D

PECORA BAYSIDE

2042 Knollview Drive
Pasadena, MD
(410) 437-5711

YUPPIE APPEAL	4
MUNCH FACTOR	3
COMFORT ZONE	3
BUD QUOTIENT	$1.75

The most popular Patapsco River watering holes are those which ring the river's basin at downtown Baltimore's Inner Harbor. From that vantage point, it's impossible to see how grand the river really is. To see the Patapsco at its boldest, you'll have to travel to the small waterfront town of Pasadena.

The most scenic panorama of the Patapsco is from the deck of the Pecora Bayside. From there, the river is at its widest - about five and a half miles - as it pours into the Chesapeake Bay, and on a clear day you can catch a glimpse of the Eastern Shore towns Tolchester Beach and Rock Hall.

HOURS: Mon.-Sun. 12-2

HAPPY HOUR: Mon.-Fri. 4-7 all drink prices discounted by 50 cents

ENTERTAINMENT: Live keyboard music throughout the summer

ACCEPTABLE PLASTIC: V, MC, AE, D

Pecora Bayside is a pleasant little Italian restaurant with a separate sit-down bar with all of the normal offerings, but what isn't normal is their pina colada. Twenty-five different coladas are served at Pecora (from Amaretto to wild cherry, with untraditional flavors such as peppermint and licorice). But the place to savor a Pecora colada is not at the bar, but out on the deck.

Enlarged and improved in 1991, the deck at the rear of Pecora Bayside comfortably seats 130 and offers both a canopied and topless section. The view from the deck, especially during the summer, is an endless parade of recreational and commercial vehicles making their way to or from the ports of Baltimore. If you want an even better riverview, you can sit out on the 80-foot pier attached to the deck. Bring you fishing rod (the pier is equipped with rod holders) and pull in a flounder or two. How many fishing piers do you know of that are served by waitresses?

To go with your Kahlua or Swiss Cocoa Almond Colada, there's a nice selection of appetizers and light fare such as crab cake sandwich, fried oyster sub, garlic bread and personal Bayside seafood pizza (and a homemade cannoli for dessert).

Plans are currently being made for a Reggae band to play summer weekends out on the deck (call for times), and by the spring of 1992, the deck will boast its own outdoor bar and large covered gazebo.

BEST TIME TO VISIT

Snag a deck chair early on a Sunday evening and stay for the moonrise over the bay.

PIRATE'S COVE

Riverside Drive
Galesville, MD
(410) 867-2300

YUPPIE APPEAL 4
MUNCH FACTOR 4
COMFORT ZONE 4
BUD QUOTIENT $2.35

It's hard to say what you'll like best at the Pirate's Cove bar, but I've narrowed it down to four: the food, the beverages, the view or the ambiance.

THE FOOD: It's nice to have the option to enjoy a full meal at the bar. But a selection of true bar foods with a surprise or two is best. There's a full complement of raw and steamed shellfish there including a raw bar combination platter for a reasonable $5.25 , but there's also hot spiced crab dip, and a fantastic offering, smoked bluefish, two healthy slabs of boneless, succulent smoked blue layered with cracked peppercorns and served with a light horseradish sauce. Ooh! And they've got eggs Benedict at the bar (try an order with a little chardonnay or white zin).

THE BEVERAGES: Wash that bluefish down with a dark beer (it's a little too intense for their wines). There are 15 beers to choose from (unfortunately, no keg brew), plus five upscale wines by the glass and a premium featured wine of the month. Rum drinkers have it made at the Pirates Cove. Eight different rums are offered, with a "Dark & Stormy," made with Gosling's and ginger beer, as the house favorite. In the winter, over a dozen spiked coffees from Irish to Dutch to Russian are ready to warm the insides.

THE VIEW: Just outside the window is the Pirates Cove marina and the West River. From April through October, the establishment sponsors Wednesday sailboat races over a four- to six-mile course. Up to 100 boaters participate each week. On Wednesdays, the Goslings and ginger beer flows like water. During the other evenings, there's plenty to see dockside. Boats costing more than your house are constantly

making their way to and from the marina slips.

THE AMBIENCE: When you take your seat at the bar, say hello to Joe, the Pirates Cove's 31-year veteran bartender. Joe knows bartending. He knows how to treat a customer, and how to get interactions started between patrons.

BEST TIME TO VISIT

Boaters and wannabe boaters should make their way down the Cove on Wednesday evenings. Those seeking more traditional entertainment (live music and dancing) should opt for Friday or Saturday night.

HOURS: Mon.-Sun. 11:30-1:30

HAPPY HOUR: Mon.-Fri. 4-7 $1.00 off all liquor drinks and domestic beer

ENTERTAINMENT: Fri.-Sat. live keyboard, dancing 8-12

ACCEPTABLE PLASTIC: V, MC, AE

RAM'S HEAD TAVERN

33 West Street
Annapolis, MD
(410) 268-4545

YUPPIE APPEAL 3
MUNCH FACTOR 5
COMFORT ZONE 3
BUD QUOTIENT No Bud

For those who take beer seriously, it just doesn't get any better than this. The Ram's Head Tavern is the Rolls Royce of brew pubs.

Only a small English-style tavern sign announces the cellar pub along a commercial strip of West Street in Annapolis. The first thing a beer lover will notice after he enters the small cellar is the number of keg sticks protruding from behind the bar. In all, there are 18 brands of draft brew ranging from Pennsylvania's Rolling Rock to Germany's D.A.B. And just when that beer lover thinks he has seen it all, he's handed a menu displaying over 130 beers from 28 countries.

HOURS: Mon.-Sun. 11-2

HAPPY HOUR: Mon.-Fri. 5-7 all drafts for $2.50 plus free hot munchies

ENTERTAINMENT: Progressive jazz via CD stereo

ACCEPTABLE PLASTIC: V, MC, AE,

Although there are such exotics on that beer listing as an $8.25 St. Sixtus Abbey Ale, a $10 Trois Monts Ale and a $12 bottle of Belgium's Chimay, the bulk of the offerings hover at or below the $3 mark.

They do something at the Ram's Head that should be done at all beer-intensive taverns. Patrons there can have a five-and-a-half-ounce sampling of any of the 18 draft beers for only a dollar (which is quite a deal considering that the majority of the draft offerings go for $3 per 12-ounce glass). As an added incentive to try something new, the tavern offers an ice bucket filled with any six bottled beers (priced $3 or less) for $15.

Warning: they don't sell Budweiser (which they refer to as the "B Word"). The only top-selling domestic lagers there are Coors, Michelob and Rolling Rock. All of the other American offerings (over 25) are microbrews.

Patrons can enjoy their brew (the place has a complete liquor selection, but who cares?) in three different locales. About 30 customers can comfortably fit in the dimly-lit main tavern, a slightly spartan mix of bare brick and hardwoods. A smaller room in the back is filled with comfortably-spaced tables. There's also an outside patio where patrons can dine and drink beneath the shade of a wisteria-covered trellis.

Shepherd's Pie is created in the Ram's Head kitchen along with a 33-ingredient chili, smoked bluefish and two dozen other curious entrees and munchies.

BEST TIME TO VISIT

The Ram's Head is a small place with a big clientele, a weekday early evening visit is a good choice.

TIMBUKTU

1726 Dorsey Road
Dorsey, MD
(410) 768-4331

YUPPIE APPEAL 3
MUNCH FACTOR 3
COMFORT ZONE 2
BUD QUOTIENT $2.35

Maryland has all kinds of bars. There are theme bars, sports bars, gay bars, yuppie bars, biker bars, hillbilly bars and redneck bars to name a few, and Timbuktu is none of those. Timbuktu is a **trencherman's bar**. People go to Timbuktu to eat and drink - a lot.

A vodka and tonic there is a six-ounce glass filled with ice and vodka, a six-ounce glass of tonic, and an empty glass. Straight shots are usually served up in snifters filled half way. For most patrons, two Timbuktu drinks is more than enough to carry them through an entire evening.

Timbuktu offers its patrons (mostly the 35-and-over crowd from the nearby office parks) a well-stocked bar featuring a well-brand, a call-brand and a premium brand from each spirit category, and two dozen different imported brews in an atmosphere that probably reminds them of their knotty pine paneled basement family rooms at home.

And then there's the food. The obligatory chunks of cheese, cauliflower and carrots are set out at Happy Hour. But setting next to the cheese and rabbit food, there will always be a large hot plate that could be filled with whole marinated, skinned and boneless chicken breasts. Or it might be crammed full of rumacki (chicken livers wrapped with bacon), which go down so well with a mug of dark ale.

Since the first half of the week is economic death for most bars, Timbuktu lures in the patrons then with some great specials. Monday there is "Lobster Nite," a 24-oz (more or less) lobster for $5.95. Tuesday is "Shrimp Nite," $5.95 for a pound of jumbo spiced shrimp. And Wednesday is "Steak Nite," where $9.95 gets the customer a 16-ounce T-bone, Porterhouse or New York Strip with veggies.

Here's a helpful hint for Timbuktu patrons who discover they've had too much to drink (an easy accomplishment there): have some bread. It's a loaf the size of a duckpin bowling ball, commendably crispy on the outside, airy on the inside, and served up hot from the oven. It's a delicious way to soak up any surplus alcohol.

BEST TIME TO VISIT

Lobster Nite or Steak Nite is always a good bet.

HOURS: Mon.-Sat. 10-2; Sun. 11-2

HAPPY HOUR: Mon.-Fri. 4-7 $1.10 drafts and free hot munchies

ENTERTAINMENT: Tues.-Sat. live key-board/vocals

ACCEPTABLE PLASTIC: All but CB

TOPSIDE INN

1004 Galesville Rd.
Galesville, MD
(410) 867-1321

YUPPIE APPEAL 4
MUNCH FACTOR 3
COMFORT ZONE 3
BUD QUOTIENT $2.50

There are quite a few waterfront taverns (but, none listed in this book) that harbor (pun intended) a"We're-giving-you-a-waterview-so-what-else-do-you-want?" attitude. Well, a non-parking lot view just isn't enough. What is enough? The Topside Inn.

A restaurant by day, the Topside transforms into a comfortable weekend piano bar at night, and a Dixieland tavern on Sundays.

Located along a quiet, wide stretch of West River adjacent to a large public dock (offering free dockage), the Topside Inn treats its patrons a great waterview from the tables and a great wood view from the bar. The ornate backbar flanked on both ends with alabaster columns was acquired, according to the owner, from the U.S. Naval Academy's Officer's Club back in the 1940s.

Over 25 bottled beers, including 10 imports and four different non-alcohols, are displayed along the backbar along with a nice selection of California varietals, including Sebastiani and Barefoot, served by the glass. During the summer, 15 frozen drinks are created behind the bar. And as many spiked coffee creations are poured when the large four-sided fireplace is active.

It's a white collar, 30-and-over clientele that occupies the bar stools at the Topside, and the drinks of choice are the super-premium selections (Absolut, Grand Marnier, Drambuie); rum creations featuring Gosling's, Myers's and Mt. Gay; and something called *Ricke's Revenge*, a secret-recipe Chambord cocktail.

No freezer-to-fryer appetizers are available to bar patrons. Lite fare there is mainly the made-from-scratch seafood munchies such as crab balls and bacon-wrapped barbecued shrimp, raw bar fare plus soft shell crab and crab cake sandwiches.

It's probably safe to say that the house piano player, Fred Loose, knows what the Topside customer wants to hear. He's been tickling the ivories there for the past 18 years, and the Topside Jammers, the nightspot's house Dixieland band, has been performing every Sunday since 1980.

HOURS: Mon.-Fri. 4-12; Sat. 8a.m.-12:30; Sun. 8 a.m.-10

HAPPY HOUR: None

ENTERTAINMENT: Fri.-Sat. piano bar 8-close; Sun. Dixieland band 5:30-9:30

ACCEPTABLE PLASTIC: V, MC, DC

BEST TIME TO VISIT

Have an early Sunday dinner at the Topside and stay for the Dixieland show.

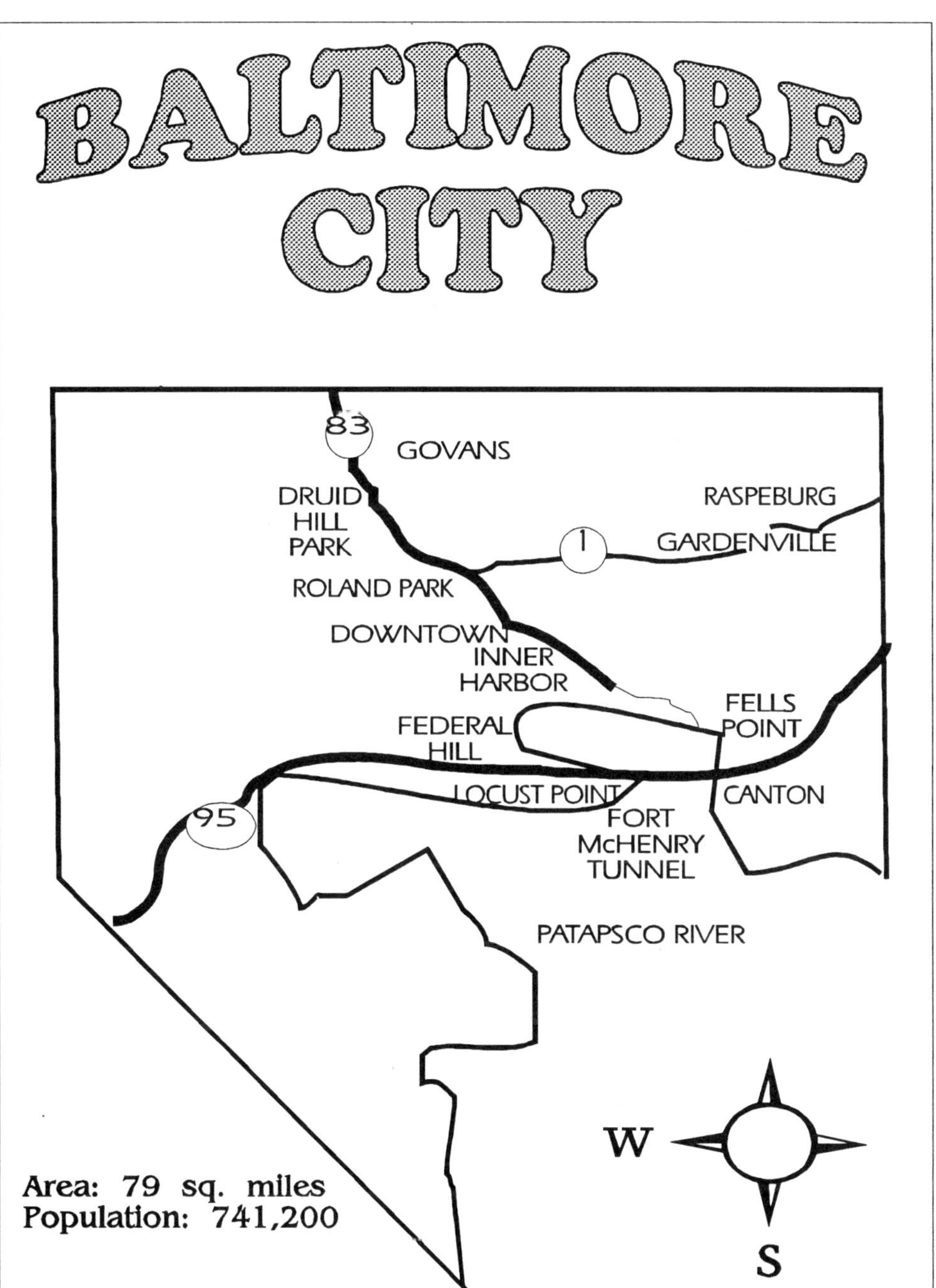
BALTIMORE
CITY
83
GOVANS
DRUID
HILL
PARK
RASPEBURG
1
GARDENVILLE
ROLAND PARK
DOWNTOWN
INNER
HARBOR
FELLS
POINT
FEDERAL
HILL
LOCUST POINT
CANTON
95
FORT
McHENRY
TUNNEL
PATAPSCO RIVER
W
S
Area: 79 sq. miles
Population: 741,200

ALONSO'S

415 W. Cold Spring Lane
Baltimore (Roland Park), MD
(410) 235-3433

YUPPIE APPEAL 5
MUNCH FACTOR 5
COMFORT ZONE 2
BUD QUOTIENT $2.00

Even sixty-three years ago, Alonso's was not a stereotypical Baltimore City neighborhood pub. In 1929, the tavern offered seven imported beers, an extraordinary number of foreign brews considering the fact that over 90 percent of the beer sold in Maryland at the time was the locally-made stuff (National Boh, American, Arrow, etc.)

Today, Alonso's is a landmark (a few years ago, a sales brochure for a nearby group of condos listed "within walking distance of Alonso's" as one of its features), and people still go there for the beer - and more.

At first glance, you'll notice something that separates Alonso's from its hundreds of city counterparts. The bar is contained behind Baltimore's only stainless steel storefront. And after you take your seat, look down under the padded armrest and you'll see the only stainless steel bar in the U.S. It's a huge oval bar setting on an Italian terrazzo floor and surrounded by paintings of famous battle scenes from the owner's private collection.

The majority of those who frequent Alonso's (students from Johns Hopkins, Loyola, and white collar types from Roland Park) are beer lovers, and their taste is reflected in the tavern's bar menu, which was constructed mainly by patron request. Currently over 100 U.S. microbrews and imported beers from 25 countries, including such rarities as Germany's Dinkel Acker, Texas' Rattlesnake, and a $30 three-liter bottle of Belgium's Corsendonk Ale, inhabit the beer list.

Alonso's boasts "Basic good food," but that's a bit of an understatement. The place has become famous for its pub fare. Their pizza is a made-from-scratch masterpiece - one of the very best in the state. And their burgers have become a Baltimore legend. Those unfamiliar with Alonso's cuisine may flinch when they read the hamburger listings in the menu, where a regular burger with tomato, lettuce and fries is priced at $5.95. What the menu doesn't state is that the "regular" burger is 16-ounces; and the jumbo hamburger (known regionally as a "meatloaf on a bun") weighs in at a pound and a half.

HOURS: Tues.-Sun. 11-2; closed Mon.

HAPPY HOUR: None

ENTERTAINMENT: Jukebox

ACCEPTABLE PLASTIC: None

BEST TIME TO VISIT

For great food and a great crowd, visit Alonso's on a Friday evening.

BALLS

200 West Pratt St.
Baltimore (Inner Harbor), MD
(410) 659-5844

YUPPIE APPEAL 4
MUNCH FACTOR 4
COMFORT ZONE 2
BUD QUOTIENT $2.25

On the roof, there sit three satellite dishes. Positioned on the walls in the three-story watering hole (and on the outside deck) are 28 studio-quality monitors and one 10-foot projection TV hooked up to 40 Bose speakers. It's **couch potato heaven**.

Unlike Baltimore's other well-known sports bar, whose major draw is customer-participation sports, Balls (full name: Balls - The All American Sports Bar) caters to those who view rather than those who do.

Utilizing those three rooftop dishes, Balls can bring in virtually every televised sports event telecast from any corner of the globe, and white-collar types fill the place to watch. Even watching the primarily redneck sporting events (stock car races, tractor pulls, professional wrestling, etc.) becomes accepted social behavior while at Balls.

Many Balls customers have become regulars because of the bar's ability to tailor the entertainment to meet the wants of the individual. Is there a Yugoslavian rugby match or a London soccer game you want to catch? Tell the bartender and he'll lock one of the dishes on the signal and feed it to one of the monitors.

If all that TV viewing works up your appetite, you're in the right place. Balls offers up a great selection of pub food featuring hoagies, Cajun chicken sandwiches, turkey reubens and some of the best seafood soups in the city. And to wash down the grub, there's Sam Adams, Bass and Moosehead on draft, plus over a dozen bottled imports and a admirably deep spirits selection.

Balls has an interior that can't help but strike an emotional chord in all first-time patrons. It's impossible to feel an ambivalence towards the decor. You'll either love it or hate it. Compared with its next door neighbor, Crickett's (featured herein), the place is positively high-tech with its brightly-colored ceramic tiled walls and bar, metal fencing and (of course) all those TVs.

BEST TIME TO VISIT

During Superbowl Sunday, the World Series, the NCAA Final Four games, the next Heavyweight Championship fight, the Indy 500, the Kentucky Derby, the Preakness, the Belmont Stakes, Hulk Hogan's rematch with Jesse "The Body" Ventura...

HOURS: Mon.-Thurs. & Sun. 11-11; Fri.-Sat. 11-2

HAPPY HOUR: Mon.-Fri. 4-7 $1.00 drafts and free hot munchies on Friday

ENTERTAINMENT: Television

ACCEPTABLE PLASTIC: V, MC. AE

BALTIMORE BREWING CO.

104 Albemarle Street
Baltimore (Inner Harbor), MD
(410) 837-5000

YUPPIE APPEAL 5
MUNCH FACTOR 3
COMFORT ZONE 1
BUD QUOTIENT No Bud

Behind the bar inside the Baltimore Brewing Company (BBC), there's a selection of spirits smaller than those found in most home bars. There's a rum there, and a whisky and a gin and a vodka, and very little else. Patrons don't come to the BBC bar to sip highballs or shoot shooters. They come there specifically to down mugs of freshly made Euro-style brew, with a .3 liter glass going for $1.90, a half-liter mug selling for $2.85, and a 1.8 liter pitcher for $8.

Utilizing such ingredients as German malts and Czechoslovakian hops, the BBC creates smooth, flavored-filled beers on the premises. Always on tap are a lager (the smoothest and lightest of the bunch), a pils (a strong and admirably bitter Czech-style beer), a marzen (malty and sweetest of the selections) and a dark lager (characteristically malty and toasty).

Dyed-in-the-wool Bud men should be warned that there's not a Budweiser (or any other commercially available beer) in the place. It's BBC beer or nothing, but that's not as bad as it may sound. Bud men should order a mug of lager and taste the difference that freshness makes.

The munchies selection at the BBC seems to have been created specifically to match up with the homemade brews. Not your ordinary pub fare, there's Crusty Cheese Bread ("topped with pureed black beans, roasted pepper sauce and goat cheese"), wild mushrooms baked in a puff pastry with gruyere, and a host of other similarly esoteric offerings. And for the traditionalists, there are half-pound burgers, BBQ chicken sandwiches, etc.

As out of the ordinary as the food and drink are at the BBC is the decor. Directly behind the bar is a massive copper cooker which is actually used in the preparation of the BBC beers, and a maze of pipes and beams dominate the ceiling. If there was something - anything - acting as divider between the pub patrons and the restaurant patrons at the Baltimore Brewing Company, though, the bar would be a much more comfortable place to kick back and enjoy some great beer.

HOURS: Sun. 4-10; Tues.-Thurs. 11:30-11; Fri. 11:30-12; Sat. 4-12; closed Mon.

HAPPY HOUR: Tues.-Fri. 4-7 $1 off .5 liter mugs, $6 pitchers

ENTERTAINMENT: Eclectic mix of tunes via CD and tapes

ACCEPTABLE PLASTIC: V, MC, AE

BEST TIME TO VISIT

Plan for an early Friday night start, and visit the BBC at 5 p.m. Take a scheduled tour of the brewery, then settle down for a mug of marzen and a grilled smoked krackauer sausage sandwich.

BANDALOOPS

1024 S. Charles Street
Baltimore (Federal Hill), MD
(410) 727-1355

YUPPIE APPEAL 4
MUNCH FACTOR 5
COMFORT ZONE 4
BUD QUOTIENT $1.90

Without the aid of gadgets or gimmick's this little Federal Hill tavern has been quietly doing everything right for years.

Although it's a four-season pub, Bandaloops really comes into its own when the mercury drops below 30. Then, the air inside is filled with the aroma of hot apple cider and the sound of a crackling blaze in the fireplace located just a few feet from the bar.

Although the place rates high on the *Yuppie Appeal* scale, all walks of life co-exist extremely comfortably at Bandaloops (the place is staffed with non-yuppie types). The backwall is brick. The backbar is a big, bold oak structure. The top of the oak bar is lined with copper and marble. And a big picture window looks out over Charles Street.

Best bets at the bar during the cold months are a "Hot Apple Pie" (the hot apple cider blended with Tuaca), a Swiss Peppermint Patty made with cocoa, or one of a dozen different spiked coffees. Another winner at the bar is Bandaloops "Frozen Irish Coffee," which won the annual "Baltimore's Best Irish Coffee" competition an unprecedented two years in a row.

But man does not live by liquids alone, and Bandaloops has been busy establishing its bar as a place for casual gourmet dining. Even a burger is not just a burger there. The "Burger Bandaloop" is a half-pound of freshly ground beef slathered with peppercorn mayonnaise. And there are similar twists on two dozen other traditional favorites including "Kudra's Fries" (fried potato wedges under melted provolone serve with a spicy sauce), "Grilled Chicken Sandwich" (sauteed breast topped with sun-dried tomatoes, mushrooms, peppers and provolone served in a warm, crispy croissant) and "Turkey Saga"(a croissant filled with smoked turkey, spinach, tomato and sage cheese smothered with champagne mustard.

Of course, the cuisine, beverages and ambiance of Bandaloops is served up year round.

But there's just something about that place in the wintertime.

BEST TIME TO VISIT

Bandaloops is the perfect spot to begin a Federal Hill pub crawl. Have a hearty meal with a frozen Irish coffee there and you're ready for the night.

HOURS: Mon.-Sun. 11:30-2

HAPPY HOUR: Mon.-Fri. 5-7 discount drinks

ENTERTAINMENT: Mixed bag of music via CD stereo

ACCEPTABLE PLASTIC: V, MC, AE, DC

BUDDIES PUB

313 N. Charles Street
Baltimore (Downtown), MD
(410) 332-4200

YUPPIE APPEAL	3
MUNCH FACTOR	4
COMFORT ZONE	4
BUD QUOTIENT	$2.60

Sometimes, following one's dream can be an expensive proposition. In February 1987, Mary Lou Brosso bought herself a downtown Baltimore bar which she insisted on converting into a straight-ahead jazz tavern. Throughout that winter and into the spring, she enjoyed a brisk lunch business, but when the sun disappeared, so did the customers. Jazz musicians played to empty seats for the first four months of the new club.

Although Baltimoreans have not been kind to the large jazz clubs, there are aficionados in Baltimore, and they slowly discovered Buddies. Today, the place fills when the music plays (Thursday through Saturday nights).

Even if you're not familiar with the Bing Miller Quartet or the Dennis Michaels Trio (Buddies' two house bands), the place is a comfortable alternative to the usual rock bars, and the music there is free (two drink minimum).

Two dozen beers (half imports) are offered at the long, inviting hardwood bar. Wine is mostly poured from Sutter Home mini-bottles, and the spirit selection is complete, with Irish Coffee as the specialty.

Mary Lou's daughter, Carole, heads a kitchen that turns out gourmet pub fare. A graduate of the Hyde Park Culinary Institute of America and currently working towards a Master Chef designation, Carole lends an artist's touch to such tavern staples as half-pound burgers and ten-alarm chili, plus she has filled the menu with things wondrous like pasta Primavera, 13 specialty sandwiches, Caesar salad, and a hot chocolate truffle sundae.

White collar types from adjacent office buildings fill Buddies during the afternoon, but at night, the place turns into a true urban melting pot. Black and white, young and old, and the rich and poor file into the upstairs bar. According to the management, the clientele there can best be described as "discerning people who can hear and who can think." For those who are jazz-illiterate but would like to know what it's all about, Buddies' customers are always glad to share what they know about the genre.

HOURS: Mon.-Sun. 11-2

HAPPY HOUR: Mon.-Fri. 4-7 2-for1 rail drinks & beer

ENTERTAINMENT: Wed. live bluegrass; Thurs.-Sun. live jazz

ACCEPTABLE PLASTIC: V, MC, AE, D

BEST TIME TO VISIT

Get there by 8:30 on a Saturday night to grab a good seat and a meal before the show starts at 9:30.

CAFE TATTOO

4825 Belair Road
Baltimore (Gardenville), MD
(410) 325-RIBS

YUPPIE APPEAL 3
MUNCH FACTOR 4
COMFORT ZONE 2
BUD QUOTIENT $2.25

Belair Road: From downtown Baltimore to two miles outside the Baltimore Beltway, it's a seven-mile commercial strip slicing through six different neighborhoods. And along that section of Belair Road there must be 35 neighborhood bars. Most of those bars are beer dispensaries filled with trophies, and so it is at the Cafe Tattoo. But there are some not-so-subtle differences between Tattoo and its contemporaries.

Cafe Tattoo offers its patrons over 100 different beers on its menu, but those are just the standard offerings. Whenever a new beer is introduced to the Maryland market, the Tattoo will have it. Recent acquisitions there include microbrews such as Red Tail Pale Ale and Anderson Valley Ale, plus Ngoma malt liquor from Togo.

For those who like their brew from a tap, Tattoo offers five: De Groen Marzen, New Amsterdam Pale Ale, plus two other imports and a house beer, Tattoo Brew.

While other bars along Belair road show off trophies displaying bowlers or pool shooters, the trophies on the backbar at Cafe Tattoo are topped with men in chef hats, and pigs. Tattoo won its trophies in national competitions with its barbecue sauce. If your idea of heaven is beer and barbecue, this is the place.

Available at the bar and at the lounge are imported baby back ribs, beef brisket and pork barbecue sandwiches, plus a barbecue beef platter all utilizing the Cafe Tattoos award-winning sauce. There's also fruit wood-smoked chicken, steamed shrimp (for only $9.75 a pound), homemade burritos and other foods that were meant to be consumed with brew.

Even though Cafe Tattoo is designed for the beer drinker, there are some surprises in the spirit selection there. Where else are you going to find a neighborhood bar offering Cynar (an artichoke aperitif), Monte Teca (tequila liqueur) and Goldwasser (German schnapps filled with flecks of 22 carat gold leaf)?

During the summer, most Tattoo patron retreat to the backyard beergarden for live entertainment or horseshoes.

BEST TIME TO VISIT

Get there by eight on Thursday for dinner in the lounge and stay for the live rock or jazz bands.

HOURS: Tues.-Sat. 4-2; Sun. 2-6 in beergarden during summer

HAPPY HOUR: Tues.-Wed. 11p.m.-midnight half-price house draft

ENTERTAINMENT. Thurs.-Sat. live rock, jazz, progressive

ACCEPTABLE PLASTIC: None

CAT'S EYE PUB

1730 Thames Street
Baltimore (Fells Point), MD
(410) 276-9866

YUPPIE APPEAL 3
MUNCH FACTOR 0
COMFORT ZONE 0
BUD QUOTIENT $1.75

Forty years ago when Fells Point was an honest port-of-call, bars like the Cat's Eye dominated that Baltimore waterfront town. It had been a sailor's bar, but the sailor's are all but gone. The few old salts that still reside in Fells Point continue to frequent the Cat's Eye during the day, but at night and on the weekends, the bar has been taken over by the white collar and college nouveau Fells Point crowd.

The Cat's Eye is a wonderfully cluttered little bar filled with mementos of earlier days. The ceiling is covered with ship's flags that were given to the proprietor by sailors to cover their bar tab. The backbar is lined with foreign currency from visiting seamen, and the walls are filled with ornate knot displays, paintings and murals by local artists.

Fells Point's only bona fide Irish Pub (they used to have a parrot trained to say "Up the Queen,"), the Cat's Eye bar has a full contingent of Irish spirits and creams but, also acting as the community's last remaining mariner's haven, there's plenty of rum to be found inside - over a dozen brands. To accommodate the hordes of landlubbers that descend after the sun goes down, the Cat's Eye has beer, and lots of it.

Guinness is drawn from the tap at 54 degrees for those who want to savor the flavor, or at 36 degrees for those who insist on cold (albeit tasteless) beer. Twelve other active taps dispense such goodies as McEwan's Scottish Ale and Washington, D.C.'s Olde Heurich. Just under 60 bottled beers (mostly imports) are also available, and the popular "lawn mower" beers such as Coors Light, long-neck Buds and Miller Lite lie buried in an ice-filled tub.

Standing-room-only crowds fill the Cat's Eye for the beer, spirits and live entertainment (a mix of Irish, classic rock and jazz) most every night, and on the weekends, even standing room is at a premium, but no one seems to mind. You'd be surprised how easy it is to meet someone when your sharing the same square foot of floor space with her.

HOURS: Mon.-Sun. 1-2

HAPPY HOUR: None

ENTERTAINMENT: Mon.-Sun. live music at night; Sat.-Sun. afternoon bands

ACCEPTABLE PLASTIC: None

BEST TIME TO VISIT

If you get there around 7 on a weekday night, you might just be able to snag one of the 15 barstools (the only seats in the place). Settle back with a couple Guinnesses (54 degrees, please) and stay for the show.

CORNER BAR

101 W. Fayette Street
Baltimore (Downtown), MD
(410) 752-1100

YUPPIE APPEAL 5
MUNCH FACTOR 2
COMFORT ZONE 4
BUD QUOTIENT $3.25

Nineteen different single malt scotches. Twenty-two different blended scotches. Fifty-four different liqueurs. Thirty-four different domestic and imported whiskies. Twenty different vodkas. Eighteen different gins. A dozen different tequilas and mezcals. Eleven different brandies. Two dozen different cognacs and armagnacs. And 54 different beers.

Welcome to the Corner Bar.

For those whose idea of a night on the town is eight Buds and four Jacks, the Corner Bar's forte will go unnoticed, and an evening there will probably cost them considerably more than at their usual Bud dispensary (see Bud Quotient). But for adults harboring a kid-in-a-candy-store mentality when it comes to liquor, the place is a joy.

Sitting at the beautiful tri-level bar, Corner Bar customers are confronted with four levels of spirits at the backbar, but even a visual scan of the bottles doesn't tell the whole story. So the Corner Bar presents the patron with a 100-page brand menu that not only lists each of the offerings, but gives a short description of each entry (e.g. St. George Pear Eau de Vie - *Five pounds of ripe, luscious pears go into your glass of this American-made "water of life")*.

At the Corner Bar, customers can have their draft (Killian's, Beck's Dark, and a trio of signature brews) by the mug (15 oz.), the half-yard (24 oz.) or the yard (42 oz.). Java drinks can be made with one of six gourmet coffees (including a Kenyan and a Kona), espresso or cappuccino. And those wanting "only the best" can get it there for a bargain. Remy Martin's Louis XIII cognac is the most expensive beverage available in the state (the stuff retails for around $1,200). The

handful of establishments that carry it sell it for between $65 and $80. The Corner Bar "gives it away" for $42 a serving.

Those who just want to finish up the day with something sweet won't be disappointed with the Corner Bar's speciality drink selection. The bartenders are well versed in over 50 frozen drinks such as Bit o'Honey, Strawberry Shortcake and a sinfully rich German Chocolate cake.

BEST TIME TO VISIT

Stop by the place during the week after a late dinner at one of the Omni's restaurants and cap the night with a liqueur that you've never tried before.

HOURS: Mon.-Sat. 11:30-2; Sun. 12-12

HAPPY HOUR: Mon.-Fri. 4:30-7:30 plenty of free hot munchies

ENTERTAINMENT: Soft rock, jazz via CD stereo

ACCEPTABLE PLASTIC: All but CB

P.J. CRICKETT'S

206 W. Pratt Street
Baltimore (Inner Harbor), MD
(410) 244-8900

YUPPIE APPEAL 5
MUNCH FACTOR 3
COMFORT ZONE 3
BUD QUOTIENT $2.25

I really want to believe all of the claims that the P.J. Cricketts Pub staff makes about the interior adornments in their place because if all of the accouterments found therein are genuine (and I have no reason to think otherwise), the place is an historical chronicle of Baltimore and beyond - with beer taps.

In 1983, the State of Maryland officially recognized the building housing Cricketts as a National Historical Site - an authentic Civil War era structure. A charred beam discovered during a later excavation there is purported to be a relic of the Great Baltimore Fire of 1904. But the best historical remnants are those found inside.

Cricketts has the greatest backbar in Baltimore, period. When the Old Astoria hotel in New York was razed in 1921, as the story goes, its lounge's backbar was rescued and smuggled to Staten Island where it served as a speakeasy centerpiece. The incredibly ornate and massive chunk of handcarved cherry was stripped and refurnished to its original state.

Other objects d'art that have found their way into Cricketts, after having been scavenged from demolished grand hotels, are its lobby's metal wall facade and glass ceiling from The Commodore in New York. And the suggestion box there began its life as a solid brass mailbox salvaged from a Philly hotel in 1915.

When spring hits Baltimore, Cricketts takes its act outside. Customers, especially on the weekends, quickly lay claim to the small tables on the large semi-enclosed patio offering unobstructed views of the city's newest arena - Oriole Park at Camden Yards.

Two dozen bottle beer brands (with Sam Adams and a couple big names on tap) complement a fully-stocked bar in the tavern, and an abundance of quality pub food is offered up. A dozen appetizers (potato boats, BBQ shrimp, etc.), and 15 sandwiches (from backfin crab cake to French dip) are available to the tavern dwellers (the place also has three separate dining rooms).

HOURS: Mon.-Fri. 11-2; Sat.-Sun 12-2

HAPPY HOUR: Mon.-Fri. 4-7 all liquor drinks 25% off

ENTERTAINMENT: DJ rock on Baltimore sporting event nights; 2-3 piece acoustic

ACCEPTABLE PLASTIC: V,MC,AE,DC

BEST TIME TO VISIT

Stop in Cricketts during an evening early in the week and avoid the crowds, or visit the place after an Oriole home game and rub elbows at the patio.

DEAD EYE SALOON

2600 Insulator Drive
Baltimore, MD
(410) 539-7784

YUPPIE APPEAL 5
MUNCH FACTOR 1
COMFORT ZONE 2
BUD QUOTIENT $1.50

The Dead Eye Saloon is just your basic urban taxidermy/waterfront pub. No other tavern in the state gives it patrons more to gawk at, both inside and out.

Inside, there must be 80 different species of stuffed game ranging from a Kodiak bear head to a caribou; from the biggest largemouth bass I've ever seen to a hammerhead shark. And a 25-foot marlin hangs precariously tail-first from the ceiling. Where there isn't a stuffed mammal head or game fish on the Dead Eye wall, there's a flag or a fern or a frigate part or a photo of Bogie.

Outside, a wraparound deck gives the patron an unobstructed view of the crafts docked at the Baltimore Harbor, and the Hanover Street Bridge, which is probably Baltimore City's most ornate span.

Though on the smallish side (a 75-person max), the Dead Eye manages to squeeze in music makers Wednesday thru Sunday. On Wednesdays, the tavern offers a country/western band, while pop-top-40 groups take over Thursdays through Saturdays.

And even though Baltimore has not been exactly gracious to Jazz clubs over the past few years, jazz bands continue to take the stage at Dead Eye on Sunday afternoons and evenings.

Although the drink of choice during the week is beer (the bar serves up a dozen different imports including draft Foster's), weekends at the Dead Eye are pretty much shooter-intensive.

Not extensive by any means, the Dead Eye's menu lists the usual barroom fare, but the prices, ranging from a buck for a hot dog to $3 for a burger, won't gash anyone's budget - plus it's all fresh and made to order.

Who says tavern proprietors are a cut-throat lot? On special occasions (Halloween, St. Patrick's Day, etc.) the Dead Eye's owner cranks up the company yacht and transports his clientele to Fells Point for an afternoon pub crawl at such notable pubs as John Stevens Ltd. and The Cat's Eye (featured herein).

BEST TIME TO VISIT

Go there early with a friend, around two, and snag the couch out on the deck. Sit back and watch the boats go by, take in the jazz and have a couple *Screamin' Orgasms* (a house specialty shooter).

HOURS: Mon.-Sun. 10-2

HAPPY HOUR: Mon.-Fri. 4-7 50-cent draft Bud & Coors Light

ENTERTAINMENT: Wed. live country; Tues.-Sat. live pop; Sun. live jazz

ACCEPTABLE PLASTIC: None

HIGHTOPPS

1700 Thames Street
Baltimore (Fells Point), MD
(410) 563-1008

If the Cat's Eye Pub is the old Fells Point, then Hightopps is the new. Chronologically speaking Hightopps is one of the newest kids on the block in Fells Point, and it does one thing that most of the old kids don't - exploit the view. Why should Fells Point be any different than any other urban waterfront night time destination spot? At the Inner Harbor, O.C. and Annapolis, tavern patrons quickly grab the window seats for that all-important waterview. But at Fells Point (a waterfront entertainment enclave) the vast majority of tavern customers are content to hide away in a dark tavern (they might as well be in Pittsburgh). But Hightopps takes it act outside.

HOURS: Mon.-Sun. 11-2

HAPPY HOUR: Fri. 4-7 $1 drafts and free hot and cold buffet

ENTERTAINMENT: Tues.-Thurs. live rock on the roof

ACCEPTABLE PLASTIC: All but D

YUPPIE APPEAL 4
MUNCH FACTOR 2
COMFORT ZONE 2
BUD QUOTIENT $2.50

Containing a sporty motif (but not a sports bar), Hightopps occupies a three-story Thames Street townhouse plus the roof of the ice cream shop next door. Two separate sit-down bars occupy the first floor, a light and unpretentious area decorated with a few neon signs and a large aerial view of Memorial Stadium. The second floor is reserved for dining, and a third-story door leads out onto Hightopps' rooftop cafe. From the deck, the view southward is the Potapsco and the waterfront industries on the opposite shore, and to the east is downtown Fells Point at the Square.

There's a big enough variety of beers (14 bottled beers and three drafts including Foster's and Bass) and a basic selection of wines, but the Hightopps bars' strengths lie in their spirits category where up to 15 specialty frozen blended drinks are offered (depending on the time of the year). Settle back on the deck with something sweet (Hightopps Cookies & Cream: Baileys, white creme de cacao, Oreo cookies, Hershey's chocolate and vanilla ice cream) or something sweet & potent (Frozen Canvass Cooler: 151-proof rum, Australian dry rum, blackberry brandy, strawberries, OJ and cream).

Fifteen deli-style sandwiches dominate the menu along with a nice selection of lite stuff, salads and burgers weighing in at eight and 12 ounces. Throughout the week, daily food specials at Hightopps really bring the cost of dining down: (Wed) half-pound burger for $2, (Mon) NY strip steak dinner for $6.95, (Tues) a full pound of jumbo steamed shrimp for $6.95.

BEST TIME TO VISIT

Any summer weekend up on the roof.

THE HUBCAP INN

6003 Belair Road
Baltimore (Raspeburg), MD
(410) 325-3450

YUPPIE APPEAL 1
MUNCH FACTOR 3
COMFORT ZONE 3
BUD QUOTIENT $1.50

The Hubcap Inn looks like all of the other jillion Baltimore City neighborhood bars from the outside. With its bare wood exterior plastered with Budweiser and Miller Lite price signs, it's the kind of place you would probably never think to visit. It's just another of those cliquish neighborhood dives with a fixed clientele, and the last person in the world they want to see enter their bar is you. Right? Wrong!

Once you get past the tacky exterior of the Hubcap Inn, located in the tiny urban community of Raspeburg, it gets a whole lot better. The interior is squeaky clean and well-lit with a long, wide pine bar. There's a classic Wurlitzer "bubbler" juke box that's been converted to CD mode. And in the back are two recent-vintage pin ball machines and dart boards. But what sets The Hubcap Inn (which took its name from its location amidst three new car dealerships) apart from its contemporaries, is what a tavern is all about - food and drink.

That's not a misprint in the Happy Hour listing below. Happy hour at the Hubcap starts at 7 (in the morning!) and runs through 6 p.m. - seven days a week. That means domestic drafts (always served in an iced 12-ounce mug) go for a half buck and bottled domestics for a dollar 11 hours a day. Aside from the usual brews, the bar serves up 40 other imports, microbrews and domestics.

The Hubcap's half-pound burgers (freshly created and cooked to order) have become so popular that the menu has recently been revised to include 15 different variations. Although the burgers are the best bet, there are over 30 other hot and cold sandwiches and subs (all freshly created) to choose from.

On Mondays, a 72-ounce pitcher of draft goes for $4. On Tuesdays, all rail drinks are a buck. Wednesday special is $1 schnapps, and Thursday is the "Hubcap Original Balloon Night" (check it out).

During the summer, you can take your brew out to the Back Seat Garden Room, their backyard patio, and indulge in some fresh pit beef or steamed crabs.

This is not your ordinary neighborhood watering hole.

BEST TIME TO VISIT

The place is going strong on Friday night by 8 p.m. According to the owner, it's not a meat market then, rather a "target-rich environment."

HOURS: Mon.-Fri. 7a.m.-2; Sat.-Sun 8 a.m.-2

HAPPY HOUR: Mon.-Sun. 7a.m.-6 $1 domestic draft.

ENTERTAINMENT: Western, oldies & top-40 via CD jukebox

ACCEPTABLE PLASTIC: None

HULL STREET BLUES

1222 Hull Street
Baltimore (Locust Point), MD
(410) 727-7476

YUPPIE APPEAL	4
MUNCH FACTOR	4
COMFORT ZONE	2
BUD QUOTIENT	$1.50

Ok. Let's say you're the type who likes to stay away from the tourist and yuppie meccas of Annapolis, Inner Harbor, Fells Point and that ilk. You like to travel off the beaten path in search of that illusive "diamond in the rough" watering hole; found among the hardcore neighborhood pubs that serve both kinds of beer (Bud and Bud Light), and where the music stops and all eyes focus in on the door when a newcomer enters (you know exactly the kind of place I'm talking about).

Buried deep down in Baltimore's Locust Point community, there's the great little Irish pub, Hull Street Blues, that has probably never played host to a Baltimore conventioneer or traveling salesman because of its distance from any hotel or white collar meatmarket.

It's a well-restored beautiful old saloon dating back over a century and filled with hardwood, brass and just enough foliage to keep it out of the fern-bar classification.

Before taking your seat at the bar, take a lap around the place. Objects hanging from the brick walls range from the requisite *Dogs Playing Poker* painting to more interesting artifacts including a hand-carved figurehead, and a huge painting of the yacht Spirit of Baltimore, which originally served as a PR sign displayed at the Baltimore docks when the Pride was being constructed. According to the owner, Hull Street Blues has been adopted as the official stopover for the Pride's crew whenever they return to their home dock.

Two dozen bottled beers are available at the bar along with five draft offerings including Sam Adams, Bass and Guinness Stout (which better be there if they want Irish Pub status). And the antique backbar supports a full contingent of spirituous beverages.

Although located in a neighborhood filled with neighborhood bars, whose specialty de la maison is pork rinds, Hull Street Blues offers up a great selection of two-fisted sandwiches filled with steamship round or Polish dogs or a crab cake or eight ounces of burger. Not that hungry? There's mussels or shrimp or stuffed mushrooms...the list goes on and on.

HOURS: Mon.-Sun. 11-2

HAPPY HOUR: Mon.-Fri. 4-7 discount drinks and free hot munchies

ENTERTAINMENT: Mix of music via CD stereo

ACCEPTABLE PLASTIC: V,MC,AE

BEST TIME TO VISIT

Happy hour is happiest on Thursdays and Fridays at around 6.

KISLING'S TAVERN

2100 Fleet Street
Baltimore (Fells Point), MD
(410) 276-9814

YUPPIE APPEAL 3
MUNCH FACTOR 5
COMFORT ZONE 2
BUD QUOTIENT $1.75

There's a precisely defined route that yuppies, college kids and other status seekers trod when they visit Fells Point. Covering portions of Broadway, Thames, Aliceanna and Fells Streets, that route is lined with taverns and pubs that fill beyond capacity every weekend night. One block away from that route is Kisling's Tavern, one of Baltimore's great bars. The only reason, I can come up with as to why there aren't Beemers and Benzs orbiting the place in search of a parking spot is that yuppies just haven't discovered it.

Kisling's is a classic "Fells Point-style" eating and drinking establishment. The long, narrow tavern is bordered on one side by a 50-foot, 30-stool bar, and on the other by seven comfortable booths.

Great beers including Sam Adams ale and lager, and Whitbread are drawn from a keg there along with four other draft selections, and 22 packaged brews are on the menu including Banks (a great little West Indies' pilsner), and 10-ounce Buds, a rarity in that section of town.

Wines at Kisling's are the full complement of Domaine St. George in the little bottles, and all manner of spirits line the backbar. But what really sets Kisling's apart from all of the other Fell's Point bars situated "off the route," is their food. The title "Baltimore's Best Tavern Food" in *Baltimore Magazine's* annual reader's poll has been awarded to Kisling's kitchen for the past two years (1990-1991).

All the stuff you would expect to find in a great tavern menu are there including a vast array of finger foods, deli sandwiches, clubs, grilled steak or chicken sandwiches and half-pound burgers. You can also kick back at Kisling's with a cold mug and a full meal at a great price. And

each night at Kisling's, there's a food promo going on that drops those prices even lower: $9.95 prime rib dinner on Tuesdays, $6.95 butterfly Cajun shrimp dinner on Wednesday, etc.

At the time this guide was going to press, a huge, bright canary yellow canopy was being affixed to the front of Kisling's tavern. Keep an eye out for it next time your in town.

BEST TIME TO VISIT

That Tuesday prime rib special is a helluva deal, and it comes with a discount priced 16-ounce mug of Sam Adam's - a great match.

HOURS: Mon.-Sun 11-1:45

HAPPY HOUR: Mon.-Fri. 3-7 $1.25 domestic beer and rail drinks

ENTERTAINMENT: Full mix of tunes via 3,000 stereo tapes

ACCEPTABLE PLASTIC: V, MC. AE

OASIS NITE CLUB

308 E. Baltimore Street
Baltimore (The Block), MD
(410) 752-7251

YUPPIE APPEAL ?
MUNCH FACTOR 0
COMFORT ZONE ?
BUD QUOTIENT $4.50

The Block: Baltimore City's most infamous real estate. It's a city landmark made up of a dozen "Show Bars" huddled one next to the other along both sides of a block and a half section of East Baltimore Street bounded to the north and east by Baltimore municipal offices and the Baltimore City Police Department.

It's the brightest and most garishly lit section of Baltimore after dark, and no book on Maryland's taverns would be complete without a brief look at The Block.

I opted to enter the Oasis for two reasons. One, it's one of the clubs that doesn't charge a cover. Two, it was the only club that didn't have some old hawker at its door daring me to step in.

Immediately upon taking my seat at the bar, which runs the length of place, this extremely large bartender asked for my order. I got a beer.

There was a girl on the long narrow stage in front of the bar. She was topless, and appeared somewhat bored as she performed her interpretive dance to the Stones' *Under My Thumb*. But she wasn't the real entertainment.

One of the other dancers, dressed in basically nothing, took a seat next to me and asked me my name. If I had thought for half a second, I would have said "Rex." But I didn't think and gave her my real name. She asked me what I did, and I told her I was a magazine editor. From then on, the scene was rather Kafkaesque. Here was this practically naked girl shaking her yahbows in my face and telling me about her favorite Dave Barry column (the one about the fishing trip and the barracuda).

After we swapped Barry stories, she asked if I would buy her a Bloody Mary. I flagged down the extremely large bartender and ordered the drink. He slid it to me and said "Twenty dollars." After a brief coughing spasm, I told him I wasn't shelling out $20.

I resumed my conversation with the dancer, and the extremely large bartender interrupted, "You can't talk to the lady if you don't buy her a drink." I offered to share my beer with her, but he said that wouldn't do.

I waved goodbye to the dancer and then to the extremely large bartender.

HOURS: Mon.-Sun. 1-2

HAPPY HOUR: None

ENTERTAINMENT: Interpretive dancers

ACCEPTABLE PLASTIC: V,MC,AE,DC

BEST TIME TO VISIT
I'll leave that up to you.

OWL BAR

Charles and Chase Streets
Baltimore (Downtown), MD
(410) 539-1355

YUPPIE APPEAL 5
MUNCH FACTOR 4
COMFORT ZONE 4
BUD QUOTIENT $2.50

This isn't a bar. It's a cathedral! If you've never been in Baltimore's Owl Bar, you're in for a treat. And if you are an Owl Bar veteran, you're in for a treat, too. The tavern has recently been completely restored to its former grandeur and, once again, it's Baltimore's most elegant watering hole.

The 90-year-old bar began its existence in Baltimore's grandest hotel, The Belvedere. To befit such a chic address, absolutely no expense was spared in its construction. The brick walls were constructed in a German rathskeller tapestry by Italian masons. The floor was laid with Italian tiles. The ceiling, 24 feet above, was given a Moorish gridwork. The windows were hand-blown lead crystal. The booths were the traditional turn-of-the-century upholstered pub benches. And the 60-foot bar and incredible backbar were made of solid mahogany.

Over the years, various owners of the Owl Bar did their best to "modernize" the facility with paint and paneling and even (gasp!) Formica. Owl Bar patrons from the mid-1950s through the spring of 1992 never knew what the place was supposed to look like until now. It's easy to pick out first time visitors to the restored bar by the expression on their face as they walk through the entrance arch.

Fourteen bottled beers - half imported - are poured at the Owl Bar supplemented by five drafts including Dortmunder Union and the local microbrew Oxford Class served up by the glass, the half-yard and yard. Blossom Hill wines are poured by the glass, but the pub menu lists a large variety of bottles selling for $14 or $17.

Super premium cordial and spirit (Grand Marnier, Drambuie, Chambord, etc.) prices drop nicely during Happy Hour, as do the spiked coffees, including their Mediterranean version with brandy and Sabra chocolate-orange liqueur.

That pub menu is 10 pages of appetizers, salads, burgers, sandwiches, Tex-Mex cuisine, pastas, entrees and desserts. Just what you would expect in a place like this.

BEST TIME TO VISIT

Get there early enough on Friday to snag one of the pub booths and have some Happy Hour munchies.

HOURS: Mon.-Sun 11:30-2

HAPPY HOUR: Mon.-Fri. 4-7 discount drinks

ENTERTAINMENT: Mix of the 50's through 70s via CD stereo

ACCEPTABLE PLASTIC: V, MC, AE

RUSTY SCUPPER

402 Key Highway
Baltimore (Inner Harbor), MD
(410) 727-3678

YUPPIE APPEAL 5
MUNCH FACTOR 3
COMFORT ZONE 5
BUD QUOTIENT $2.25

Where should you go when you go to Baltimore's Inner Harbor? Each of the nightspots facing the mouth of the Patapsco river rate a "5" on the *Yuppie Appeal* scale, a "3 to 4" rating for *Munch Factor,* and similar high scores in the *Comfort Zone.* And there's not a big disparity in those waterfront watering hole *Bud Quotients.* Which brings us down to why most visitors opt to visit the Inner Harbor clubs in the first place - a beer, a burger (or variations thereof) and an urban waterfront view.

Elevate yourself to the 13th floor of the Inner Harbor's Hyatt Regency and you can have a view of the harbor and far beyond - assuming, of course, you luck into a windowside table. And there are commanding views of the harbor proper from the various Light Street and Pratt Street Pavilion clubs. Then, there's the Rusty Scupper.

Setting all alone on the south shore of the Inner Harbor, the Scupper offers its patrons a wide, third-story wraparound deck surrounding its Topsider Lounge. There, visitors have the choice of lounging harborside with a panoramic view of the neon area (from the MD Science Center to the Scarlett Place condos, and everything in between), or settling back on the deck's south side where the scene shifts dramatically (freighters, warehouses and, of course, the Domino Sugar sign).

Food and drink are offered up in abundance and good variety (with one notable exception). Since the lounge is a paean to summer, it offers up a dozen frozen libations, both spiked and benign (did you know that a rumless pina colada tastes remarkably similar to its high-proof counterpart?). A good sampling of brews is also available with eight foreign jobs and eight U.S. entries. But if draft is your choice, you don't have one. Only one brew, Michelob, pours from the tap.

"Scupper (yuppie-style) Pizza," with chicken breast and monterey jack, heads the pub food listing at the Scupper. And there's the omnipresent Buffalo wings, plus half-pound burgers, all manner of sandwiches, shrimp and even calamari (fried squid bits).

BEST TIME TO VISIT

Get there early enough to pick and choose from the 18-foot buffet (only offered on Fridays) then take your seat on the deck and take in the view.

HOURS: Mon.-Sun. 11-2

HAPPY HOUR: Mon.-Fri. 5-7 discount drinks and half-price snack menu

ENTERTAINMENT: Contemporary and top-40 taped music

ACCEPTABLE PLASTIC: V,MC,AE,DC,D

SCARLETT COVE CAFE

200 S. President Street
Baltimore (Inner Harbor), MD
(410) 783-8760

YUPPIE APPEAL 3
MUNCH FACTOR 2
COMFORT ZONE 4
BUD QUOTIENT $2.50

For a Baltimore harbor visit without the crowds, there's just one place to go. Located on the quiet side of the Harbor, the Scarlett Cove Cafe has all of the benefits of a Harborplace tavern without any of the hassle. Those who have ever tried to find a parking spot within a half mile of Harborplace on a Friday or Saturday night will especially appreciate Scarlett Cove, one of the harbor's newest restaurant/taverns located on the ground floor of the condominiums of the same name. Just pull up to the cafe's front door for free indoor valet parking.

Have you ever wondered what the grand old serving bars (like the one in the Owl Bar) looked like when they were brand new? The 40-foot Italian marble-topped bar inside the Scarlett Cove is destined to become a classic. The wood used in its construction was made from a single mahogany tree (so each panel would contain matching grain patterns).

Directly across from the bar are a row of tables offering an open view of the Patapsco, the National Aquarium and the other tourist meccas along the waterfront.

Although the Scarlett Cove has the look of a high-dollar yuppie emporium and is located inside one of Baltimore's most expensive waterfront condo complexes, prices there do not hover in the upper atmosphere. Only two of the 20 luncheon entries available at the bar and lounge break the two-digit barrier. The veal, seafood and fowl dishes average around $7.50, with appetizers such as shrimp in garlic sauce (the house specialty) going for $5.95.

All of the familiar brews (about 20 in all) are poured at the bar, and the three 50-foot rows of spirits along the backbar is one of the most complete Inner Harbor selections. As would be expected, a lot of wine is consumed at the Scarlett Cove. Six selections from wineries including Casal Thaulero and Chalk Hill are served by the glass, and the bottled wine list contains over 40 names ranging from a $12 Gallo white zin to a $120 Dom Perignon. Don't worry, most wine prices are in the teens.

BEST TIME TO VISIT

Friday nights at Scarlett Cove Cafe have the best crowds, and it's the best night of the week at the Inner Harbor to indulge yourself with valet parking.

HOURS: Mon.-Thurs. 11-11:30; Fri.-Sat. 11-2; Sun. 12-11

HAPPY HOUR: Mon.-Fri. 5-7 discount drinks and munchies

ENTERTAINMENT: Fri.-Sat. keyboard player

ACCEPTABLE PLASTIC: All

SISSON'S

36 E. Cross Street
Baltimore (Federal Hill), MD
(410) 539-2093

YUPPIE APPEAL 5
MUNCH FACTOR 5
COMFORT ZONE 2
BUD QUOTIENT $2.00

Sisson's beer menu is arranged the way a well-rounded beer menu should be - by type, instead of by country of origin. Over 30 beers (mostly imports) are grouped on their menu under the categories "Pale Ales," Wheat Beers," "Pilsners," "Stouts & Porters," etc. And there are some great beers represented including Maisel's Hefe-Weizen, Corsendonk Monk's Ale, and Whitebread. But if you go to Sisson's and order one of those imports, you've made a big mistake.

For three years, Sisson's has been brewing its own beers which can be described with a host of adjectives ranging from "delightful" to "incredible." Each of those in-house beers are handmade in small batches resulting in rich, highly drinkable beverages that have amassed a huge and loyal following.

Although Sisson's Marble Golden Ale and Stockade Amber Ale are regular entertainers at the little Federal Hill tavern, Brewmaster Hugh Sisson is constantly surprising his followers with new entries. Over the past couple of years, Sisson patrons have been treated to over 15 different specialty brews such as "Redweiser," a grand weise (wheat) beer highly infused with raspberries, and Old Yeates Irish Red Ale (IRA).

One thing all of these beers have in common is freshness, and that's no small factor in beer quality. Although a small number of super-exotic brews respond well to aging, beer is meant to be consumed the moment it leaves the brewery, and it is at Sisson's.

With beer that good, Sisson's doesn't need another drawing card to keep its bar filled, but their food offerings are every bit as good as their brew. An ever changing menu of Cajun and classic American cuisine is offered up at the bar (the list is much too extensive to list here). Here's a match made in heaven: a bowl of Sisson's gumbo (thick, black and fiery) and a pint of Stockade Amber Ale. Pub food doesn't get any better than that.

There is a down-side to Sisson's (although I'm sure the proprietors don't see it as one). The great beer and great food there attracts great crowds. And on Friday and Saturday evenings, taverngoers are squeezed three-deep at the bar.

HOURS: Mon.-Sat. 11:30-2; Sun 10:30-1

HAPPY HOUR: Mon.-Fri. 5-7 discount drinks and drafts, free wings

ENTERTAINMENT: Wide mix of music via CD stereo

ACCEPTABLE PLASTIC: V,MC,AE,D

BEST TIME TO VISIT

You're best chance to grab a barstool at Sisson's is on a weekday evening or a Saturday afternoon.

THE TELL TALE HEARTH

1145 Hollins Street
Baltimore (SoWeBo), MD
(410) 234-0880

YUPPIE APPEAL 3
MUNCH FACTOR 5
COMFORT ZONE 2
BUD QUOTIENT $2.50

Not that long ago, Southwest Baltimore contained some of the meanest streets in Maryland. Slowly, very slowly, it's residents have been reclaiming their neighborhood a block at a time. Today, Southwest Baltimore (known locally as SoWeBo) resembles 1960's Georgetown, 1970's Federal Hill, and 1980's Fells Point. SoWeBo has transformed into a Baltimorean Bohemia, the city's largest artist's enclave, and The Tell Tale Hearth is a perfect complement to the revived area.

Year round, the Hearth's walls display the works of the local artists. Each year, entries from 10 art shows are given a four- to six-week showing inside the corner bistro with the life-size (and life-like) wooden sculpture of Edgar Allen Poe reclining against the jukebox as the establishment's only permanent display.

Twenty-three beers are up for grabs at the Hearth, including some good draft offerings like Sam Adams, Rolling Rock and dark Dortmunder. And for a neighborhood bar, the wine selection is fantastic: five reds, five whites and a blush (mainly French and Australian products) are served by the glass.

From a circular brick wood-burning oven in the Hearth's kitchen come some of Baltimore's (make that Maryland's) best pizza, which can be topped with such goodies as jerked or blackened chicken, gorgonzola and clams. Don't forget to specify your garlic intensity to the server: "Vampire" (no garlic), "Healthy" (lots of garlic) or "Immortal" (tons of garlic {go for it}).

That pizza alone would be reason enough to head for The Tell Tale Hearth, but this little tavern has a big menu filled with 20 hot sandwiches and as many en-

tree offerings (nothing over $10) of Italian and Caribbean origin. Author's hint #1: for something completely different, try a platter of the Hearth's sweet potato fries with some honey mustard on the side, or a side of their home-style onion rings doused with the great house hot sauce.

Author's hint #2: park your car alongside the Hearth before an O's game, walk to the stadium, then return for a pizza and a brew or two.

BEST TIME TO VISIT

Tuesday nights are the quietest and most relaxed, and your best chance at a window seat. If you think you've got talent, try Wednesday and grab the mike.

HOURS: Mon.-Sun. 11-2

HAPPY HOUR: None

ENTERTAINMENT: Wed. open mike; 2nd & last Tues. of the month poetry reading

ACCEPTABLE PLASTIC: V, MC, DC, CB

TIO LOCO'S CANTINA

1061 S. Charles Street
Baltimore (Federal Hill), MD
(410) 752-2258

Just when I thought I'd seen all the euphemisms possible for men's and ladies' room (pointers and setters, cowboys and cowgirls, buoys and gulls, etc.), I'm confronted with the bathroom doors at Tio Loco's Cantina: *WORMS - TACOS.* I chose Worms. Lucky guess.

Tio Loco's is a bar with a good attitude, and if you don't have one when you walk in, you will after a couple shots of the cantina's specialty. It's Baltimore's premier tequila bar serving up every brand of cactus juice (yeah, I know tequila comes from the blue agave, not a cactus) available to Maryland retailers, 35 in all, from the cheapest (which still burns 10 minutes after you've drank it) to the ultra primo stuff (which goes down like Kool-Aid).

HOURS: Mon.-Sat. 1-1; closed Sun.

HAPPY HOUR: Mon.-Fri. 4-7 discount drinks and drafts

ENTERTAINMENT: Rock, progressive music via CD stereo & tapes

ACCEPTABLE PLASTIC: V,MC

YUPPIE APPEAL 5
MUNCH FACTOR 1
COMFORT ZONE 2
BUD QUOTIENT $1.75

Tequila at Tio Loco should be consumed thusly: dump the cheap stuff in a margarita or sunrise (a Hussong's margarita is such an incredible waste of money). Drink the medium-priced tequila with a bottle of cuervesa (preferably Negra Modello or Dos Equis). And savor the good stuff with salt and a chomp of lime.

For the beer & tequila aficionados, Tio Loco's presents 75 different brews from 13 different countries and 35 tequilas (well over 2,500 combinations to try). And of those 75 beers, 10 different brands are drawn from the tap including DeGroen's marzen (from the Baltimore Brewing Co. [featured herein]), D.C.'s Olde Heurich, and New Castle's English nut brown ale. They also have a draft you see very little of - Bulmer's Woodpecker Cider. Try some mixed with Guinness Stout for a curious Black & Tan.

A Foosball table and a regulation dart board are on hand for those so inclined. And there's a bit of food available: burritos, quesadillas, and nachos for a few bucks.

Restaurant employees who bring their pay stubs to Tio Loco's on Wednesday get a two-for-one deal on the great selection of drafts. And Monday is "Movie Nite," free flick, free dogs, free chips & salsa and draft for a dollar.

BEST TIME TO VISIT

Get their Friday or Saturday evening before 7 and lay claim to a seat. After the Cross Street Market closes, the cantina fills to the brim.

WATERFRONT HOTEL

1710 Thames Street
Baltimore (Fells Point), MD
(410) 327-4886

YUPPIE APPEAL 5
MUNCH FACTOR 1
COMFORT ZONE 3
BUD QUOTIENT $2.50

There's no longer a hotel at the Waterfront Hotel, but the bar that served the hotel patrons from 1917 through 1955 remains as perhaps the most historically significant watering hole in Fells Point.

In the first floor of the second oldest brick house ever built in Baltimore City, you'll find the Waterfront Hotel Tavern. Originally, a sea captain's home, the structure served as a ship's store and a pre-Civil War real estate office before beginning it's tenure as a hotel during the Civil War.

When the hotel's bar was built in 1917, it was a pre-Art Deco affair made of glass block and brick. The current owners of the hotel used the thick pine doors of the 33 obsolete hotel rooms to completely panel the bar. Above the bar are lighted glass transparencies of antique Dr. Pepper and Pepsi signs, and the original stained glass that graced the front of the original hotel bar remains.

But what really makes the Waterfront Hotel bar inviting is the tavern fireplace, Fells Point's largest, at the far end of the adjacent lounge, which contains an ever-changing exhibition of local art works. During the colder months, the management keeps a bonfire going in the hearth.

Also during the winter, the best light fare is available in the tavern - raw bar selections including steamed and raw Chincoteague oysters, cherrystones clams, and mussels.

The entire upstairs restaurant menu is available to patrons of the hotel tavern and lounge. Heavy on the seafood side, the appetizers are all shellfish and shrimp entries. And there's French onion soup, fresh spinach salads plus a freshly concocted soup du jour, but no traditional pub fare.

Most patrons come to the hotel tavern during the weekdays just to enjoy a drink or two in quiet historic surroundings, but during the weekend nights the Waterfront Hotel tavern (like all Thames Street taverns) becomes a mob scene, as it transforms from a dark and quiet retreat to a yuppie/college place to be.

BEST TIME TO VISIT

Drop by the Waterfront Hotel on a Sunday afternoon during the cool and cold months for a fireside seat and a quiet drink.

HOURS: Mon.-Sun 11-2

HAPPY HOUR: Mon.-Fri. 4-7 discount drinks

ENTERTAINMENT: Thurs.-Sat. small acoustic bands

ACCEPTABLE PLASTIC: All but D

WEBER'S ON BOSTON

845 S. Montford Avenue
Baltimore (Canton), MD
(410) 276-0800

YUPPIE APPEAL	5
MUNCH FACTOR	3
COMFORT ZONE	3
BUD QUOTIENT	$2.65

Don't believe everything you read on a menu. In an effort to add an extra dimension to their establishments, owners like to stick those small historical essays about their place inside their menus. Unfortunately, these essays often haven't as much as a toehold in reality.

One prominent downtown Baltimore tavern claims that their signature draft brew was concocted from an exotic century-old recipe discovered by the men excavating the tavern's foundation. When, in reality, their beer is the same generic brand offered by 100 other Maryland pubs.

On the first page of Weber's menu, it states that the place dates back 70 years, when it served as a speakeasy and a gambling parlor. I find that claim hard to dispute, because the tavern today is a fantastic homage to the Roaring '20s.

Located along the Canton waterfront (Baltimore's newest yuppie-intensive community), Weber's has a backbar that's a 15-foot by 30-foot slab of hand-carved mahogany. The floors are bare hardwoods. The walls are brick. The ceiling is covered with an ornate stamped tin shield. And slowly spinning cast-iron ceiling fans get their juice from a single motor incorporating two exposed 40-foot fan belts. About the only item out of character in this historically-correct bar is the computerized cash register.

Though offering up a great liquor selection, along with Sam Adams and Bass on draft, Weber's forte could well be its wine list. While most nightspots are routinely retailing wines at three and four times their wholesale cost, Weber's somehow manages to hold the prices on their listing of boutique and select wines way down. As an example, a $26 (wholesale) Veuve Clicquot French Champagne (tasty stuff) goes for $47.

Formidable finger foods are also for sale at Weber's bar including all manner of shrimp and shellfish, along with such untraditional offerings as smoked salmon, beer cheese, hot crab dip with pita pieces, and "Weber Wings," a grand alternative to the hackneyed upstate New York variety.

HOURS: Mon.-Sun. 11:30-2

HAPPY HOUR: No defined happy hour, but sporadic specials

ENTERTAINMENT: Contemporary music via CD stereo

ACCEPTABLE PLASTIC: V,MC,AE

BEST TIME TO VISIT

Weber's is wall-to-wall yuppies on the weekend. For best results, try the place on a Wednesday or Thursday evening.

WHISTLE STOP

Penn Station
Baltimore (Downtown), MD
(410) 727-5671

YUPPIE APPEAL 4
MUNCH FACTOR 2
COMFORT ZONE 2
BUD QUOTIENT $2.50

They're called "Captive Audience" bars, and they can be found in places where there is no competition. A good example are the half dozen Host lounges at Baltimore Washington International airport. There, the bars offers only 12 brands of liquor, three brands of beers and one wine brand, and drink prices start at $3.75 for the beer and soar to $5.25 for a martini.

The Whistle Stop is another example of a captive bar; those waiting for a train at Baltimore's Penn Station have the option of having a drink there or not having a drink at all. But the place doesn't take advantage of its environment. Instead it looks and feels like a small and comfortable neighborhood bar.

During the week, the Whistle Stop caters mainly to Baltimore commuters making their way to or from D.C., but on the weekends, the place fills with American vacationers and Europeans on holiday, many of whom get their only impression of Baltimore from the station tavern.

To accommodate the European travelers, the Whistle Stop offers up a more than commendable selection of European bottled beers (including seldom-found brands from France and Germany) even though most foreigners opt for exotic brews like Bud and Coors (they can get Kronenbourg and Fischer LaBelle at home).

As well stocked as the Whistle Stop's beer case are the liquor shelves and the menu. There, patrons can indulge themselves with a pate platter ($4.95) or some hot Italian sausages ($3.25), or they can target their gastronomic urges toward strictly American cuisine such as chili, cream of crab soup, or a bobboli-crusted pizza topped with backfin.

Framed blow-ups of black & white photos of Baltimore, circa 1900, serve as the main interior adornments at the Whistle Stop. Just recently, the management there, in an effort to attract non-travelers, has been bringing in live entertainment (two and three-piece acoustic) on the weekends.

BEST TIME TO VISIT

Visit the tavern on an early Sunday evening when there is plenty of nearby parking, and a good chance to meet up with an Aussie or Swede anxious to talk about his home, and learn more about Baltimore.

HOURS: Mon.-Fri. 11:30-9; Sat.-Sun. 12-10; stays open for late trains

HAPPY HOUR: None

ENTERTAINMENT: None

ACCEPTABLE PLASTIC: V,MC,AE

YOUNG BIN

412 N. Howard Avenue
Baltimore (Downtown), MD
(410) 752-5992

YUPPIE APPEAL 0
MUNCH FACTOR 0
COMFORT ZONE 5
BUD QUOTIENT $3.25

Jay Ro is a veep at a local Korean liquor distributorship, and when he's called on to entertain visiting Korean businessmen and ship captains, he takes them to Young Bin.

Ro explained that Seoul nightclubs come in three classifications: low class bars, middle class bars that mainly cater to American servicemen, and upper class clubs for Korean men only. And Young Bin is the closest example of the upper class Korean establishment in Maryland.

"At those upper class bars in Korea, you don't have a waitress, you have a hostess who stays with you during your entire visit," Ro explained. "And it's not unusual for four men to spend $2,000 a night - and that's not including the $200 tip for each of the hostesses."

They keep it dark at Young Bin. The only lights are those above the well-stocked service bar. I learned that 95 percent of the spirits at bar are just for show. Patrons at Young Bin drink Chivas Regal, Johnnie Walker Red, or Remy Martin VSOP, and very little else.

Less than two minutes after Jay and I took our seats at one of the small tables, two Korean women bearing coasters sat down beside us. "We have to buy them drinks," whispered Ro. "They expect that." They liked cognac.

For the next two hours, our hostesses lit our cigarettes, poured our drinks (there, you can buy liquor by the bottle), told us about themselves, asked us about ourselves, drank cognac, and laughed at our jokes (even though I had this gnawing feeling that they weren't really getting all of the punch lines). And we danced with our hostesses to the music provided by a one-man band playing mostly Korean pop songs with a few Sinatra standards thrown in.

The munchy selection at Young Bin was on the meager side. The choice was apples or dried squid. We opted for the squid which turned out to be tan and paper thin, tasting like salty chicken with the texture of naugahyde.

Our two-hour stay at Young Bin set us back just under $200.

HOURS: Wed.-Mon. 9 p.m.-2
closed Tues.

HAPPY HOUR: None

ENTERTAINMENT: Every night a one-man electronic band

ACCEPTABLE PLASTIC: V,MC,AE

BEST TIME TO VISIT

Sundays are the busiest nights at Young Bin and there may not be enough hostesses to go around, so to get the full flavor of the place, go on a Friday night around eight.

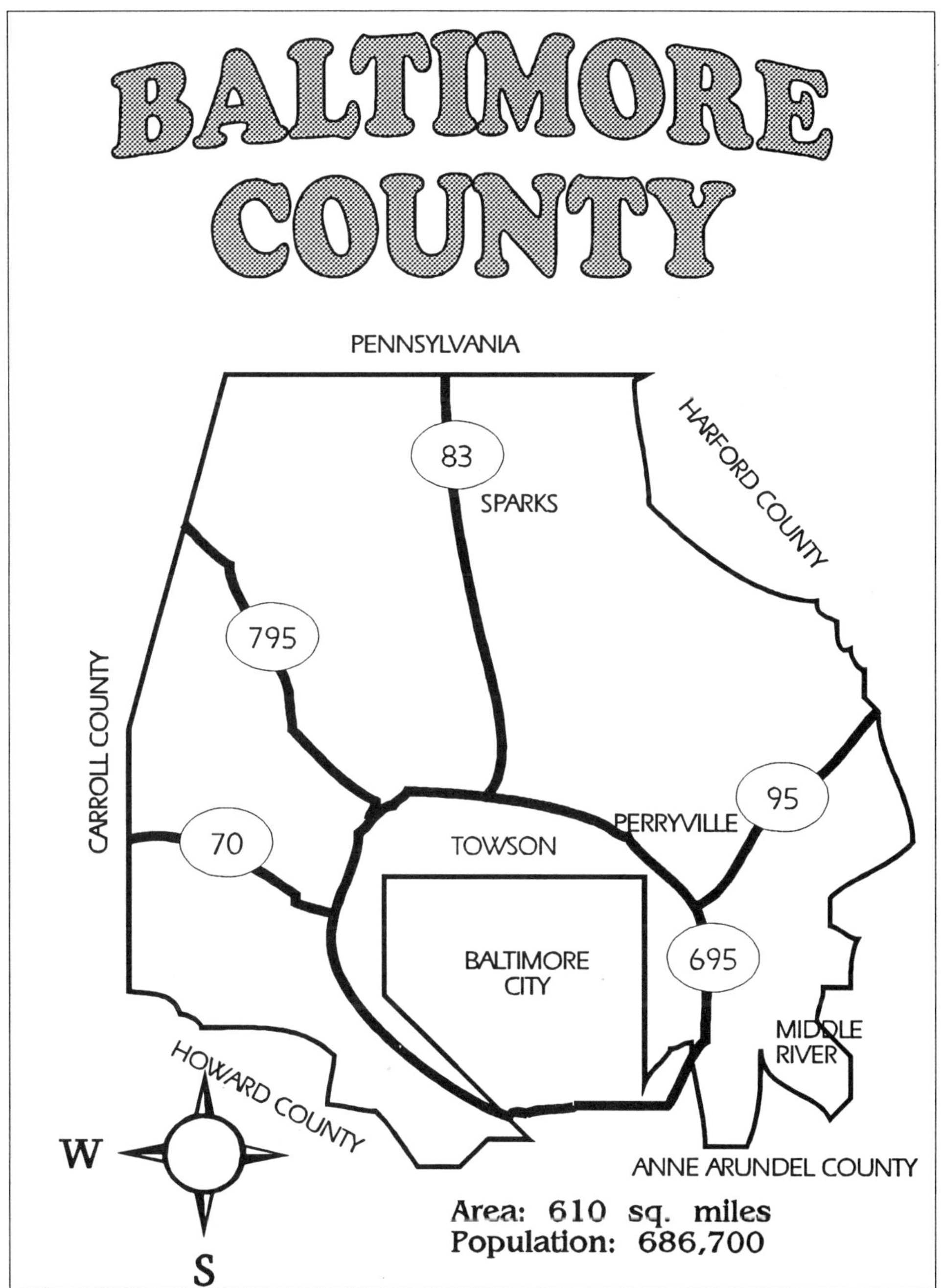
BALTIMORE
COUNTY
PENNSYLVANIA
83
SPARKS
HARFORD COUNTY
795
CARROLL COUNTY
95
PERRYVILLE
70
TOWSON
BALTIMORE
CITY
695
MIDDLE
RIVER
HOWARD COUNTY
W
S
ANNE ARUNDEL COUNTY
Area: 610 sq. miles
Population: 686,700

DRIFTWOOD INN

203 Nanticoke Road
Middle River, MD
(410) 391-3493

YUPPIE APPEAL	2
MUNCH FACTOR	3
COMFORT ZONE	2
BUD QUOTIENT	$1.75

Basically, there are two types of urban waterfront bars - white collar & no collar. The taverns along the Annapolis waterfront, for example, were created for the jacket and tie (or at least a polo shirt) crowd. On the other end of the waterfront watering hole spectrum is the Driftwood Inn whose only dress requirement is shoes (but don't worry if you come there shoeless, the management will find you a pair of flip-flops). Come to think of it, the only other difference between the Driftwood Inn and its yuppie counterparts is the amount of money it takes for a visit.

Located along Hopkins Creek, a serene and picturesque branch of Middle River, the Driftwood Inn offers it's bar and lounge patrons a great waterview without waterview prices. The most expensive drinks are the specialty beverages which include over 75 different frozen blender concoctions in the summer, and build-your-own spiked coffees in the winter. Both seasonal selections go for $3.50.

Only Bud is drawn from a tap, but the major Dutch and Mexican bottled beers are all there along with a choice of non-alcoholic brews. And a surprisingly large collection of wines (from Taylor, Charles Krug and Folinari) are served by the glass. Not quite as surprising is the availability of 30 different wine coolers.

During the weekdays at the Driftwood, there's always a grand special from the kitchen. Weekly deals include a full pound of 16-count (big boys) shrimp and a fresh ear of corn for $6.95. And on a good Thursday night, the Driftwood kitchen cranks out over 400 pounds of king-cut prime rib, an enormous slab of meat and veggies for $11.95.

An entire page of the four-page menu is devoted to finger foods and such, with breaded mushrooms, homemade onion rings and cheese covered fries selling for two bucks or less. The next menu page describes six seafood soups (beginning at $1.25) and 27 sandwiches headed by the Driftwood Burger, a 10-ounce monster with the works for $5.25.

Those downtown diner prices coupled with a waterside locale make for a nice destination.

HOURS: Mon.-Fri. 11-2; Sat. 8-2; Sun. 8-12

HAPPY HOUR: Mon.-Fri 4-7 discount drinks and hot munchies

ENTERTAINMENT: Fri.-Sun. (summer) top-40 bands

ACCEPTABLE PLASTIC: V,MC,AE

BEST TIME TO VISIT

Motorists from Westminster and boaters from Annapolis make their way to the Driftwood on Sunday evenings.

MILTON INN

14833 York Road
Sparks, MD
(410) 771-4366

YUPPIE APPEAL 5
MUNCH FACTOR 1
COMFORT ZONE 2
BUD QUOTIENT $3.50

It may be a little more expensive than your garden variety pub, but you get what you pay for at the Milton Inn's tavern.

Located in the heart of Maryland's horse country, the structure that houses the Milton Inn has been standing for over a quarter of a millennium, which makes it older than any building standing in Baltimore City. Originally a stage coach stopover, the manor served as the Milton School for Boys (later, the Milton Academy) from 1847 to 1895. Among its most famous (or infamous) students were Joseph L. Holt, the prosecuting judge for the conspirators in the Lincoln assassination, and the Milton School's most well-known resident, John Wilkes Booth.

Today, the Milton Inn is an award-winning establishment known nationally for its gourmet cuisine, and its small tavern is the perfect stopover for a sip of port or a nip of scotch.

Twelve beers are offered at the tavern, but this isn't a beer bar. It's a place to enjoy a glass of wine. Wine Critic Robert Parker is a regular at the Milton Inn (he loves the chef's rendition of soft shell crab) and the wine-by-the-glass listing is the type one would expect to find in an establishment frequented by America's most noted wine expert. A revolving list of varietals includes a dozen selections (mostly boutiques) along with over 20 fortified wines from a $3.50 glass of Fonseca ruby port to a $20 serving of vintage Taylor Fladgate 1977.

The Milton Inn's tavern is also the place to enjoy a sampling from a selection of 12 premium blended and single malt scotches or a dozen different cognacs ranging from a $7 V.S.O.P. to a $75 snifter of Remy Martin's finest - Louis XIII.

There are no chicken fingers or onion rings at the Milton Inn tavern, but the entire restaurant menu is available to the tavern patrons. Meal-in-themselves appetizers include such creations as grilled lamb tenderloin with lentil chili and tortilla crisps, and an asparagus & shrimp bisque.

If there ever was a special-occasion tavern, this is it.

BEST TIME TO VISIT

Try the place on a winter weekday afternoon when you'll have a chance to wander through the old mansion and surrounding gardens.

HOURS: Mon.-Fri. 11-12; Sat.-Sat. 5-2; Sun. 5-9

HAPPY HOUR: None

ENTERTAINMENT: Modern & classic jazz via CD stereo

ACCEPTABLE PLASTIC: V,MC,AE,DC

PERRY INN & PUB

9654 Belair Road
Baltimore, MD
(410) 529-1544

YUPPIE APPEAL 3
MUNCH FACTOR 4
COMFORT ZONE 3
BUD QUOTIENT $1.75

When times are tough and money is tight, it's nice to know there's a neighborhood pub to take sanctuary; a no-frills kind of place where a beer and a burger can be bought for the price of a Coke downtown.

But what if you don't have a neighborhood bar in your neighborhood? There's always the Perry Inn & Pub. They've taken the concept of a neighborhood pub and merely expanded on the it. Like how? Like draft beers for a half dollar daily during Happy Hour. Like a half pound of steamed shrimp for only three bucks (that's a hell of a deal) on Mondays, and there's a free taco bar and $2.50 pitchers of draft all night on Thursdays. And every Wednesday, all beer in a can goes for $1.50 from four until closing.

Perry Inn's fully stocked bar and beer selection easily accommodates most patrons, but the management there insists on expanding the scope of its customers' palates. Each month, the place features and promotes a new upscale West Coast wine at an affordable price. A recent example was Domain St. George chardonnay or cabernet sauvignon for just $2.50.

And here's something else you won't find in your stereotypical neighborhood bar: a wine selection featuring over 10 good wines (Rodney Strong, Robert Mondavi, Geyser Peak) by the glass, plus a selection of champagne splits (half bottles).

Patrons at the Perry Inn take their seats at the bar on some of the most comfortable barstools in Baltimore, and listen to jukebox tunes (country/western and rock - but mostly c/w) during the week and c/w or top-40 tunes spun by a DJ on the weekends.

Appetizers served up at the bar range from mozzarella sticks accompanied with homemade marinara to mussels Florentine. For the extremely hungry, there's a 16-ounce (four quarter pounders in one) burger for $4.25, and for the true carnivore, there's a pound slab of raw beef on a bun for $3.50. Eighteen other selections round out the sandwich selection.

Pretty good stuff for a neighborhood bar, don't you think?

HOURS: Mon.-Sun. 11-2

HAPPY HOUR: Mon.-Fri 4-6 50-cent drafts, $2.50 pitchers, free munchies

ENTERTAINMENT: Fri.-Sat. DJ country or rock

ACCEPTABLE PLASTIC: All

BEST TIME TO VISIT

Don't miss the Friday Happy Hour buffet giveaway.

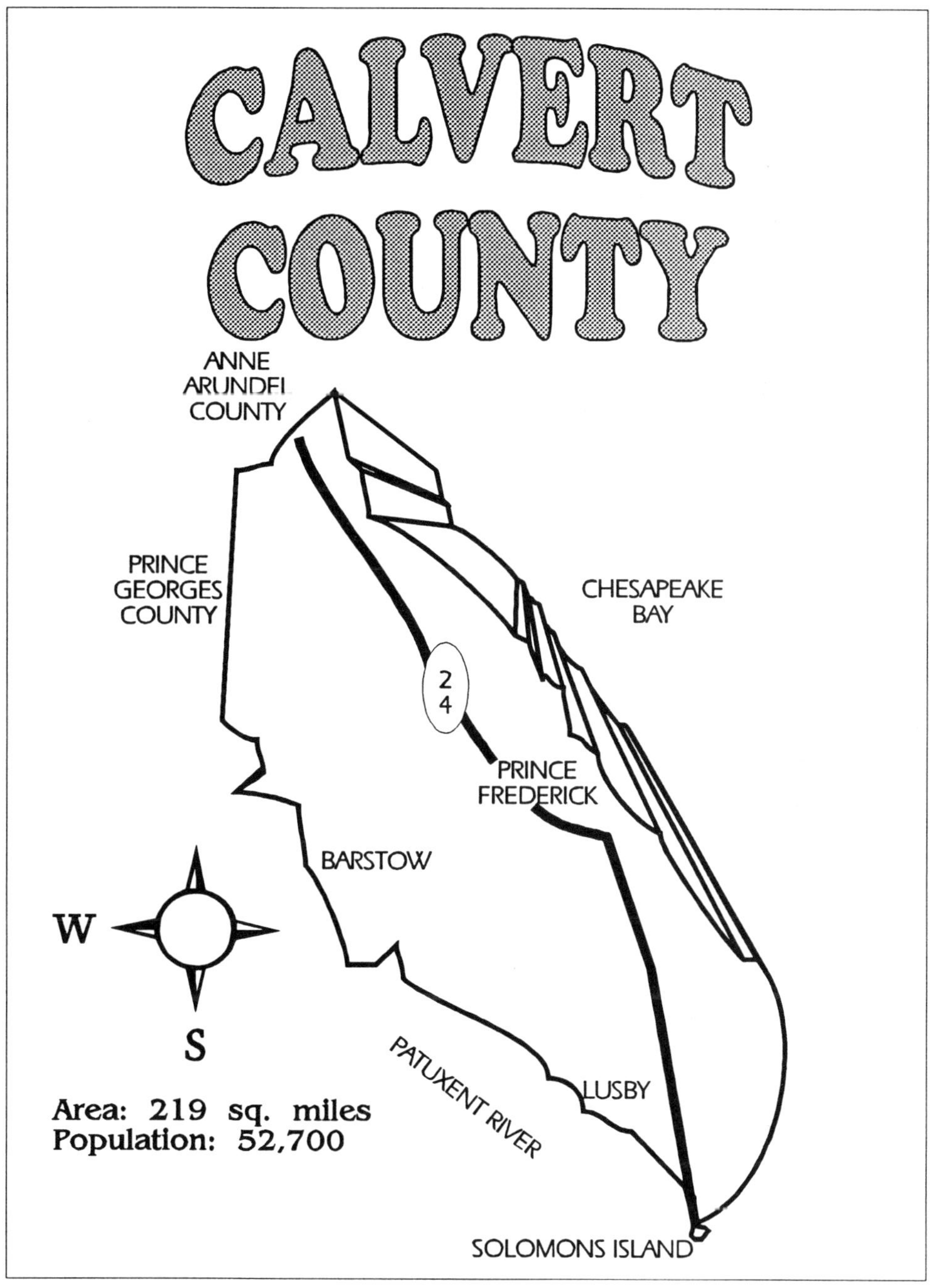
CALVERT
COUNTY
ANNE
ARUNDEL
COUNTY
PRINCE
GEORGES
COUNTY
CHESAPEAKE
BAY
24
PRINCE
FREDERICK
BARSTOW
W
S
PATUXENT RIVER
LUSBY
Area: 219 sq. miles
Population: 52,700
SOLOMONS ISLAND

COUNTRY DOCKS

6992 Hallowing Point Lane
Barstow, MD
(410) 535-3989

YUPPIE APPEAL	3
MUNCH FACTOR	0
COMFORT ZONE	3
BUD QUOTIENT	$1.75

Now here's something you don't see every day in Maryland: a waterfront country-western nightclub.

Two years ago, three Southern Maryland men who had met at a country dance class decided to build their own dance hall. With virtually no capital, the three, along with 20 friends, transformed a former VFW hall situated at the foot of the Upper Patuxent bridge into Country Docks.

The left half of the building houses the Swingin' Door Dance Hall, a clean and classy nightclub constructed primarily with doors. The huge dance floor, booths, tables, and benches are all recycled doors. And the walls, paneled with the wood from a nearby razed barn, display horse collars, cattle skulls, antlers and such donated by patrons. A string of "traveling lights" surrounds the ceiling above the dance floor.

Country Docks was built for serious country-western dancing. Tuesdays nights in the dance hall are reserved for clogging classes. On Wednesdays, it's beginner's dance classes on such steps as line dances, the country waltz and the Texas Two-Step. Specialty dances (El Paso, Wooden Nickel, etc.) are taught on Thursdays, and on Friday and Saturday nights, everyone shows up in their finest Stetsons and western apparel to show what they've learned to the tunes of bands like Gold Dust, City Slicker and Bustin' Loose.

Non-dancers can find plenty of room to listen to the music in the adjoining Honky Tonk bar or out on the deck overlooking the river and the bridge.

During the warmer months, the musicians and dancers do their thing outdoors on the deck and the 400 square foot outdoor dance floor.

They don't drink that foreign beer at Country Docks. Brews there are three domestic drafts and 10 bottled beers (all of the Buds and Millers). Forget wine, but there are plenty of coolers. And they never run low on Bacardi, V.O. and Jack.

Country luaus and beach parties are staged on Sundays along the 200-foot sandy shorefront.

HOURS: Tues.-Thurs. 3-10; Fri. 3-2; Sat. 12-2; closed Mon.

HAPPY HOUR: Tues.-Fri 4-6 discount drinks

ENTERTAINMENT: Fri.-Sat. live country/western

ACCEPTABLE PLASTIC: None

BEST TIME TO VISIT

It all comes together on Saturday night at Country Docks, but if you plan to stop by then, reservations (made as early as possible) are a must.

NAUGHTY GULL PUB

Lore Road
Solomons Island, MD
(410) 326-GULL

YUPPIE APPEAL 3
MUNCH FACTOR 3
COMFORT ZONE 3
BUD QUOTIENT $2.00

Most summer visitors to Solomons Island do the same thing. They park their car and set off on foot along Solomons Road where they pass all but one of the major island food and drink establishments. The one place that they miss is the Naughty Gull. And that's a shame.

Geographically speaking, the Naughty Gull is not on Solomons Island, but, technically, Solomons Island is no longer an island. The Gull is located a few hundred feet north of the island proper along the quiet little inlet of Spring Cove.

The P-shaped bar inside the Gull sits a few feet higher than the partially partitioned dining room giving the bar patrons not only a small degree of privacy, but an unobstructed view through the wall of windows facing the marina and cove beyond.

Like most other Solomons Island establishments, the entire contents of the menu is available barside, but the prices and contents differ considerably. I've seen luncheon specials presented at the bar such as a stuffed double pork chop (the size of a duckpin bowling ball) with all the trimmings for under five bucks. And here's why. Due to its location, away from the tourist's beaten path, the Naughty Gull has established itself as a local's establishment, and tourists lucky enough to stumble into the place are going to get the most for their money.

They're also going to get the best beer selection in town. Over 15 imports and microbrews, plus another 15 domestic brews are available. And no other S.I. tavern has a larger spirit selection than the Gull. Four varieties of wine by Sebastiani and Fetzer (better than average house brands) are also on the menu for just $2.75 a glass.

It's a quieter and slightly less hectic environment there than at its counterparts, but the place is jammed nonetheless on the weekends.

Author's note: I've had bigger, more elaborate, and pricier burgers, but I've never had a better burger than the one created recently at the Naughty Gull.

BEST TIME TO VISIT

To get the most out of the Naughty Gull, visit the place during the week. On the weekend's there's live acoustic music, but seat availability is at a premium.

HOURS: Mon.-Sun. 11-12

HAPPY HOUR: Mon.-Fri. 4-6 discount drinks and food specials

ENTERTAINMENT: Fri. small acoustic bands

ACCEPTABLE PLASTIC: V,MC

SOLOMONS PIER

Main Street
Solomons Island, MD
(410) 326-2424

YUPPIE APPEAL 4
MUNCH FACTOR 2
COMFORT ZONE 3
BUD QUOTIENT $2.25

No summer resort area along the Western Shore is more well-known than Solomons Island, and no Solomons Island establishment is more recognizable than Solomons Pier.

Jutting out more than 100 feet over the Patuxent River at it's confluence with the Chesapeake Bay, no other Island restaurant/lounge offers up more water views than this one.

During the summer, the bar at Solomons Pier is a meeting place for both tourists and locals of all ages (over 21, that is). There, they have a choice from three domestic drafts, a half dozen of the standard imports, and a complete liquor selection from which the place creates what they modestly refer to as the greatest Bloody Mary around. But they also have a selection of seven different wines to sample a glass at a time, two different bottled waters and two non-alcohol beers from which to choose.

Group members who announce to the bartender their designated driver status will receive free sodas and other N\A drinks during their stay. And that's an important point.

Only one road leads in and out of the tiny island and, especially during the summer, the local police lay in wait at that entrance/egress point. During the late hours, pitchers of ice water are set up at the bar to be consumed by customers planning to drive off the island.

Although the entire menu selection is available barside, most patrons opt for selections from the appetizer list: sweet & spicy Honey BBQ Wings, zucchini or mozzarella sticks, nachos, and great homemade onion rings to name a few.

At the far end of Solomons Pier, there sets a huge, uncovered deck surrounding the "Gazbar," a full-service gazebo bar. The view from the deck is, as you would expect, fantastic, especially in the evening while the sun is setting behind the Thomas Johnson bridge.

There's a DJ spinning rock & roll almost every night during the summer except Fridays, when Rock 97.7 sets up its remote studio for a night of music and contests (air guitar, best joke, etc.).

HOURS: Mon.-Sat. 11-2; Sun. 9:30-12

HAPPY HOUR: None

ENTERTAINMENT: Tues.-Sun. DJ rock; Fri. live FM remotes

ACCEPTABLE PLASTIC: All

BEST TIME TO VISIT

If you like crowds, Friday and Saturday nights fill the bill. And weekday early evenings there are for those who just crave a room with a view.

TIKI BAR

Main Street
Solomons Island, MD
no phone

YUPPIE APPEAL 4
MUNCH FACTOR 0
COMFORT ZONE 3
BUD QUOTIENT $2.50

To most Marylanders, the phrase "Opening Day," has something to do with the Baltimore Orioles, but to Southern Marylanders, "Opening Day" has something to do with mai tais.

On the third Friday in April, all hell breaks loose on Solomons Island as the Tiki Bar starts a new season. Last spring, over 1,500 Tiki fans made the annual pilgrimage to the island's entertainment establishment (with an SRO capacity of less than 300). Not only was the 1992 Opening Day throng the biggest in the Tiki's history, more of the bar's signature drink was consumed on that day than ever before. One hundred and ninety seven gallons of mai tais were produced and consumed during the Tiki's 1992 opener.

Solomons Island's only open air bar (as opposed to taverns with adjoining deck or gazebo bars), the Tiki was designed after the watering holes indigenous to the Florida Keys. The roof extends over the entire floorspace, but walls and windows are nonexistent. It's strictly a fair-weather bar.

There's no draft beer and very little of the imported stuff, and only one brand of wine is sold, because beer and wines just can't compete with the specialty drinks created at the Tiki. Those who come there come for the mai tais, bright red, bittersweet and powerfully potent potables pre-made in five gallon batches. And they come for drinks named *Kokomo* (Nassau Royale, Myers's rum, Malibu rum, grenadine, pineapple juice & o.j.), *Cajun Margaritas* (standard-recipe drinks using tequila and triple sec that have marinated overnight with jalapeno peppers), the Tiki's famous Bloody Marys and a half dozen other exotic concoctions.

The Tiki's food menu is a bit more simplistic - free popcorn. The place goes through over 150 pounds of unpopped popcorn each week.

From the bar and surrounding tables, there's a great view of Solomons Cove & harbor, and throughout the bar are maritime and Caribbean artifacts (strings of sponges, shark jaws, loggerhead turtle shells and carvings) donated by current and former customers.

BEST TIME TO VISIT

The Tiki Bar fills way beyond capacity on Saturday evenings, but if you get there before four, you might just grab onto a table you can call your own.

HOURS: Mon.-Fri. 4-1:30; Sat.-Sun. 2-1:30; mid April to mid Oct.

HAPPY HOUR: None

ENTERTAINMENT: Oldies, reggae, Florida sounds via tapes

ACCEPTABLE PLASTIC: None

VERA'S WHITE SANDS

1200 White Sands Drive
Lusby, MD
(410) 586-1182

Wouldn't it be great if there was a tavern where you could sit at the bar and enjoy a huge day-glo blue "South Pacific" cocktail topped with a paper umbrella, fan and pineapple ring without looking like a total dweeb? Well, you can at Vera's White Sands. In fact, it's expected there.

In other bars in other sections of Calvert County, the drink du jour may be Jack & Coke or Seven & 7, but at Vera's the perennial favorites are the Kon-Tiki (grapefruit juice, light & dark rums and pineapple juice), Peacock Tail (tall pina coladas spiked with Myers's rum), Orchid, White Sands Sunset, Banshee, and a $5 "Mystery Drink."

HOURS: Tues.-Fri. 5-11; Sat.-Sun. 12-12; closed Mon.

HAPPY HOUR: None

ENTERTAINMENT: Piano bar every evening

ACCEPTABLE PLASTIC: V,MC

YUPPIE APPEAL 3
MUNCH FACTOR 0
COMFORT ZONE 2
BUD QUOTIENT $2.25

As a first-timer at Vera's you're likely to chuckle as you approach the place from the parking lot. Surrounded by palm and banana trees (real ones) is this huge pink structure with the word "Aloha" emblazoned on the wall. But the real weirdness doesn't begin until you walk through the door.

It looks like a Pier One with tables. But look closer. The stuff (and there's a lot of stuff) scattered from floor to ceiling in Vera's is the real McCoy. The place is crammed full on one-of-a-kind artifacts from all over the world.

Vera, a 1930's starlet and owner of this strange nightclub overlooking a beautiful stretch of St. Leonard's Creek, has filled her establishment with Italian marble statues, English musket-loader rifles, African ceremonial spears, Siamese temple guard dogs, ornate mahogany Hawaiian king thrones, plus a record-size clam shell (attested by the Guinness book), the actual brass bridge-to-engine signaler from the Mauritania, and a diving helmet presented by Prince Philip.

And there are hundreds of other strange and wondrous pieces (check out the petrified boar's head) to peruse.

Ten beers are available at the bar, but they're the beers you can get anywhere. This is the place for a blue, green or international orange drink shaded by a paper umbrella.

Although the bar in Vera's White Sands is just for drinking (if you want food, you must repair to the dining room), a visit there is a must - trust me.

BEST TIME TO VISIT

Plan a stopover at Vera's on your next sojurn to Solomon's Island this summer.

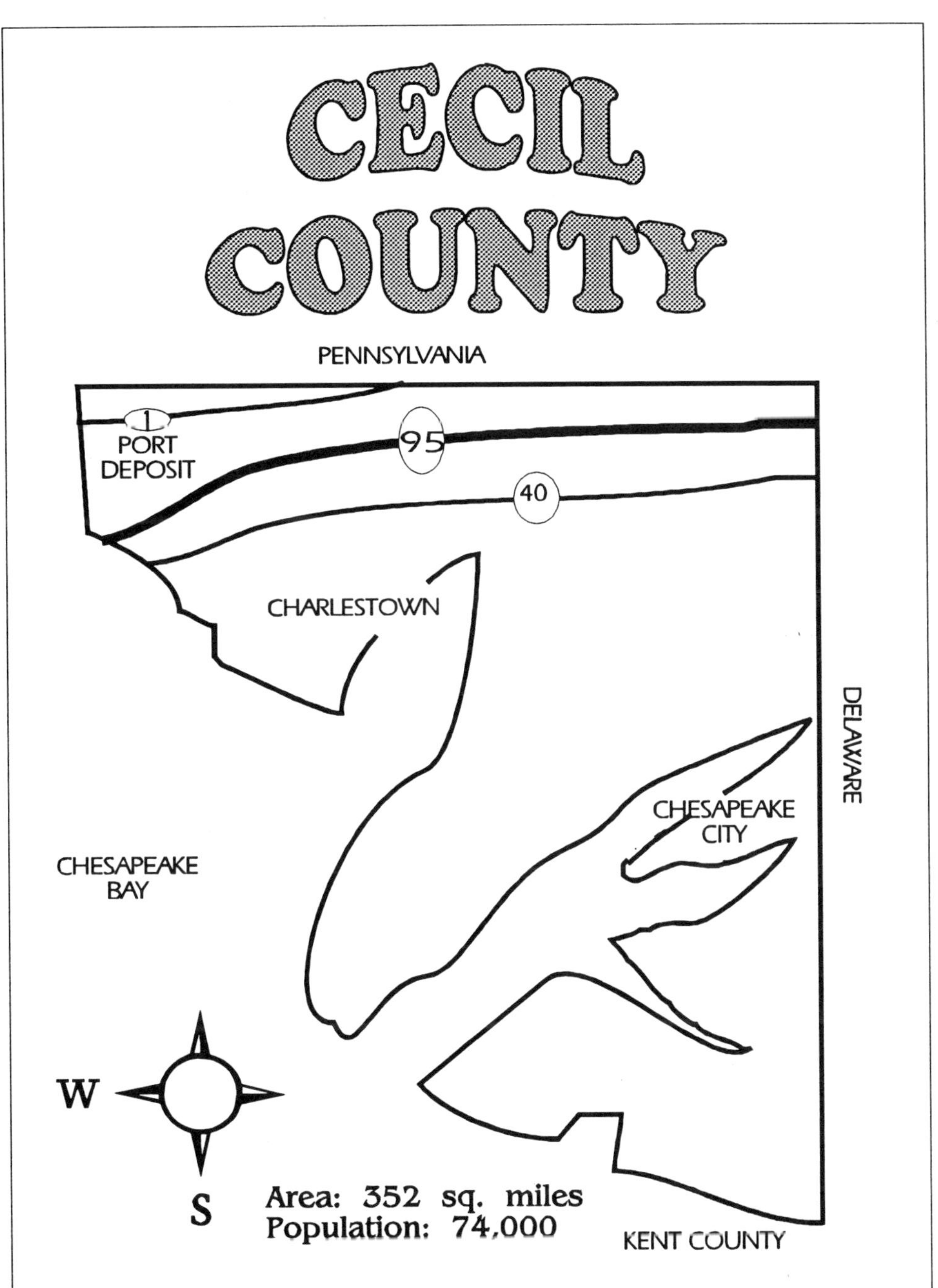
CECIL COUNTY
PENNSYLVANIA
1
PORT DEPOSIT
95
40
CHARLESTOWN
DELAWARE
CHESAPEAKE CITY
CHESAPEAKE BAY
W
S
Area: 352 sq. miles
Population: 74,000
KENT COUNTY

DOCKSIDE YACHT CLUB

604 Second Street
South Chesapeake City, MD
(410) 885-5016

YUPPIE APPEAL 4
MUNCH FACTOR 1
COMFORT ZONE 2
BUD QUOTIENT $2.25

There are two ways to view the big ships that ply the Chesapeake and Delaware Canal. You can enjoy the view from the bar or table at Schaefer's Canal House (featured herein), or you can go topside at the Dockside Yacht Club.

Located almost directly across the canal from Schaefer's Canal House restaurant, the Dockside offers a slightly less formal venue for viewing the happenings along the manmade waterway.

On the first floor, there's a small L-shaped bar secreted away from the canalfront windows. Above the backbar, MTV plays from a small television, and munchies are severely limited (chips and dip is it). That's about all that's available to visitors seeking a brew at the Dockside in the off-season. But in the summer, all kinds of good things begin to happen there.

A huge rooftop deck comes to life at the Dockside with the approach of summer. Capable of handling up to 180 patrons at a time, the bi-level deck is filled with umbrella-topped tables, plus it has its own bar (bigger than the one downstairs).

The view from the Dockside deck is tremendous. There, visitors can take in a much wider visual sweep of the canal and bridge than patrons inside the Canal House, but the Dockside is positioned further from the canal (along a service inlet) and the ocean liner crossings are slightly less dramatic there than they are from the vantage point at Schaefer's.

There may not be much grub at the Dockside's downstairs's bar, but up on the deck there's a raw bar featuring moderately-priced shellfish and spiced shrimp.

Liquors and liqueurs are abundantly stocked at the deck bar, but beers are mostly the area big sellers (Bud & Coors Light). Maybe this summer they'll have Heineken.

Since the Dockside is located off of the canal proper, it has room for dozens of moorings and, during the summer, an average of 250 pleasure boats can be seen coming and going.

HOURS: Wed.-Sat. 11-11; Sun. 1-10; closed Mon.-Tues.

HAPPY HOUR: None

ENTERTAINMENT: Sat.-Sun. small acoustic bands during the summer

ACCEPTABLE PLASTIC: V,MC,AE

BEST TIME TO VISIT

Almost any sunny day during the summer is a best bet. The proprietors say that the summer crowds are liveliest from 2 until 8 on Saturdays.

HARBOR HOUSE

200 Cherry Street
Northeast, MD
(410) 287-6800

YUPPIE APPEAL 4
MUNCH FACTOR 2
COMFORT ZONE 3
BUD QUOTIENT $1.90

Have you ever wondered what the beginning of the Chesapeake Bay looks like? I mean the northernmost terminus, the source of the Bay. Well, that spot (where the North East River pours into the Chesapeake) is the scene from the deck at the Northeast Harbor House.

Perhaps the nicest aspect of the Harbor House is that, even in the summer, it's not overrun by hordes of tourists searching for anything as long as it's happening on the water. That's not to say that the Harbor House's deck and inside bar doesn't fill to capacity, especially on July 4 when fireworks are launched from a barge anchored a few yards from the place, but the crowds there are made up of Cecil Countians and boaters docked at the adjacent marina.

Though equipped to entertain and comfort patrons year round (the inside bar comes equipped with its own small lounge filled with leather chairs and complete with corner fireplace), the Harbor House shines brightest in the summer.

From the bartenders come blended drinks in 16 different flavors. And, on summer Sundays, the band takes it act outdoors on the deck, which is equipped with it's own fully-stocked sit-down bar.

The half-dozen best-selling imported beers (Heineken, Corona, etc.) are served at the Harbor House bars, along with four domestics from the tap. All of the familiar spirits are there, and if you ask for the house drink, you'll get a "Cocaine Cocktail," which is almost as insidious as it sounds: Kahlua, Frangelico, Amaretto, Baileys and vodka served on the rocks (I wonder what's sweeter: that drink or Karo syrup?).

Their pub food menu is a well-conceived melange featuring all manner of seafoods, but also including burgers, Buffalo wings, mesquite chicken and (they say they've made this famous in northern Maryland) onion loaf, a concentrated chunk of onions and batter sliced with a knife and eaten like pate.

BEST TIME TO VISIT

From 2 until 7, there's live rock & roll on the deck on Sundays until Labor Day, if that's your thing. But if you can make it up there during the week, you can have a large portion of that deck to yourself for sitting back with a blackberry daiquiri and watching the boats go by.

HOURS: Mon.-Thurs. 11:30-12; Fri.-Sat. 11:30-2; Sun. 11:30-10

HAPPY HOUR: Mon.-Fri. 4-6:30 free munchies

ENTERTAINMENT: Fri.-Sat. small acoustic bands in lounge; Sun. on deck

ACCEPTABLE PLASTIC: All but AE

MARKET STREET CAFE

315 Market Street
Charlestown, MD
(410) 287-6374

YUPPIE APPEAL	4
MUNCH FACTOR	3
COMFORT ZONE	2
BUD QUOTIENT	$1.50

The "designated driver" (DD) concept has taken a firm hold in Maryland. More and more thinking tavern owners have adopted a DD program where a member of a group of visiting patrons receives free non-alcohol drinks during the course of the night to insure a safe trip home. The Market Street Cafe goes most DD programs one better. The designated driver who brings a group of five receives free soft drinks, plus a free meal.

Tucked away in the small community of Charlestown (if you found the place on your first try, it was luck), the Market Street Cafe is the type of establishment normally found situated in urban upper-middle class neighborhoods. Once a thriving hotel, back when Charlestown was the site of numerous public beaches and a huge amusement park, the blue building at the south end of town now serves as a modern pub and restaurant with all of its history still intact.

Pictures of the hotel in its heyday adorn the walls in the tavern along with dozens of artifacts of a half-century ago. There's also a nautical motif mixed in. Charlestown is the nearest Chesapeake Bay point of entry for a large number of Pennsylvania boaters, most who frequent the tavern.

All the beers you would expect to find in a rural tavern (Bud, Pabst, etc.) are, of course, in the coolers, but there's also a great selection of imports and microbrews from which to select. How about a nice Bitburger Pils or a Dock Street Amber?

From the tavern's kitchen comes a half-dozen variations on the burger, hoagies filled with steak or a couple crab cakes, plus salads and stromboli, pizza and pastrami, and a selection of fried finger foods for a buck or two. And whatever the $2.99 daily special happens to be in the new restaurant addition, it's also the special in the tavern. There are also plenty of small tables in the Market Street Cafe's tavern from which to enjoy a dozen steamed crabs in the summer.

An evening at the Market Cafe is the chance to experience one of the few remaining unspoiled Maryland upper shore towns - in style.

HOURS: Mon.-Sat. 11-12; Sun. 1-10

HAPPY HOUR: None

ENTERTAINMENT: Oldies jukebox

ACCEPTABLE PLASTIC: V,MC

BEST TIME TO VISIT

Get to Charlestown in the late afternoon and mingle with the boaters at the cafe.

SCHAEFER'S CANAL HOUSE

208 Bank Street
Chesapeake City, MD
(410) 885-2200

YUPPIE APPEAL 4
MUNCH FACTOR 2
COMFORT ZONE 4
BUD QUOTIENT $2.00

You're sitting at the bar, and quietly sipping on a Raspberry Coffee (Baileys, Kahlua, Chambord and hot coffee topped with fresh whipped cream drizzled with raspberry Kijafa) when an excited murmur begins at the restaurant end of Schaefer's Canal House. People start rising from their chairs and make their way towards the wall of windows facing the Chesapeake and Delaware Canal (which is less than 40 feet away). You look out the window to see the entire landscape is changing. Is an eclipse taking place? What was once a rural waterfront scene filled with piers, boat houses and small white homes is now just a slow moving wall of solid grey. This is the reason people from all over the East Coast make their way to Schaefer's - to watch the mammoth oceangoing vessels squeeze their way through the canal, which links the upper reaches of the Chesapeake Bay to the Delaware River.

It's an incredibly awesome sight to see. And during the summer, the canal hosts five or six of those massive vessels daily. Between liner crossing, the canal is a beehive of activity filled with pleasure craft, fishing boats and tugs.

Summertime is, by far, the time to visit Schaefer's. Besides the above mentioned feast for the eyes, there's a feast for the ears on the patio. Each summer the Canal House presents a genuine Caribbean steel band from Wednesdays through Sundays out on their patio (complete with its own bar and grill). And speaking of feasts...

At the bar, the entire restaurant menu is available; including seven different seafood appetizers in the afternoon, and an even dozen in the evening. But you might just want to sit and munch the fresh-baked pretzels and cheese sticks (best ones you'll ever taste) presented for free (the menu items are good but they aren't cheap).

There's an admirable selection of wines by-the-glass, including several fine champagnes, at the Canal House bar, as well as a fully stocked bar. But the beer listing, unfortunately, is on the skimpy side (three imports, three domestics).

BEST TIME TO VISIT

Stop by Wednesday through Saturday in the summer for the steel band and your best chance to watch one of those huge ships lumber by.

HOURS: Mon.-Sat. 11-11; Sun. 1-10

HAPPY HOUR: None

ENTERTAINMENT: Wed.-Sat. Caribbean steel band during the summer

ACCEPTABLE PLASTIC: V,MC,AE

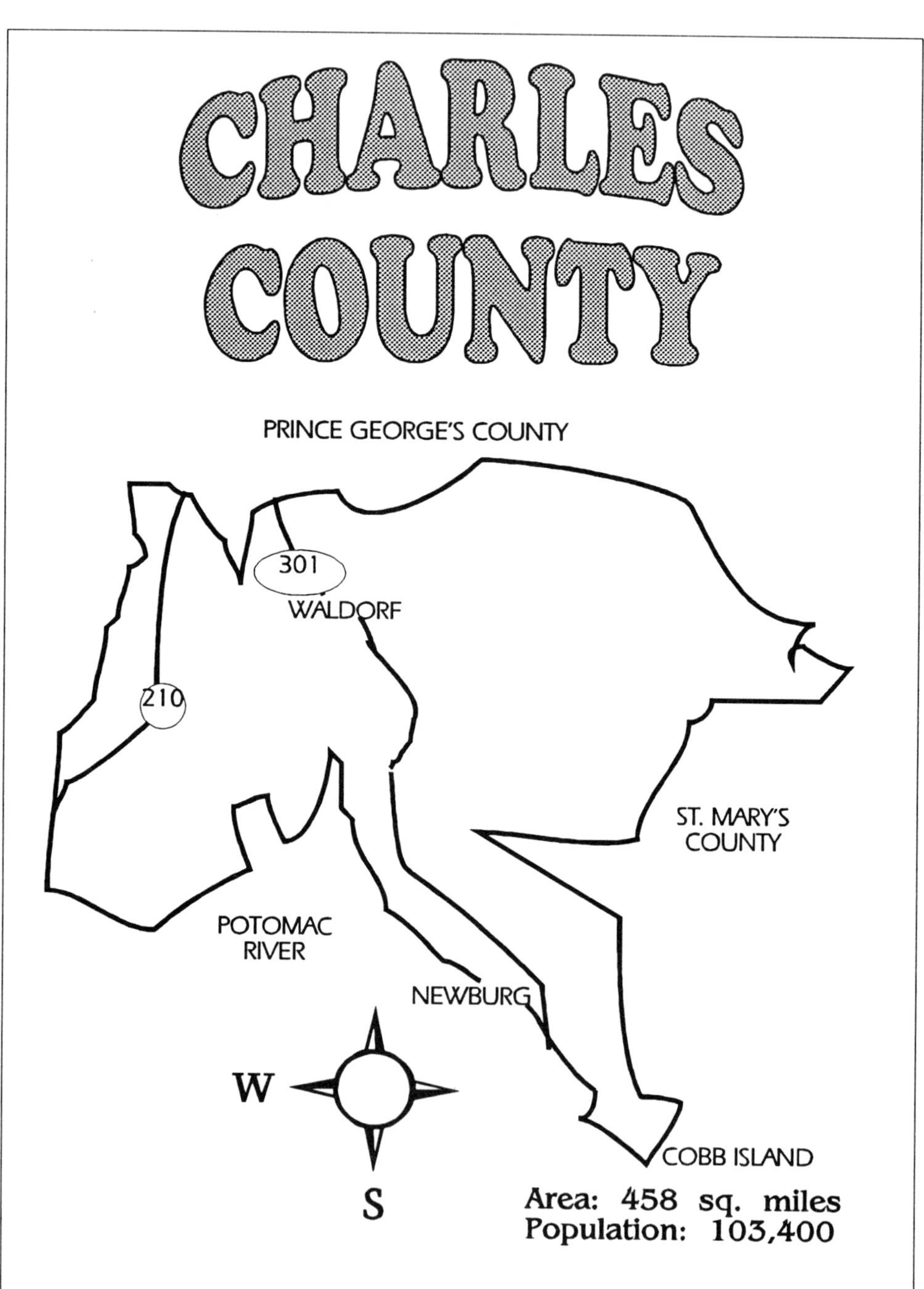
CHARLES
COUNTY
PRINCE GEORGE'S COUNTY
301
WALDORF
210
ST. MARY'S
COUNTY
POTOMAC
RIVER
NEWBURG
W
S
COBB ISLAND
Area: 458 sq. miles
Population: 103,400

BRAVO

St. Charles Towne Center
Waldorf, MD
(301) 870-6604

YUPPIE APPEAL 5
MUNCH FACTOR 4
COMFORT ZONE 4
BUD QUOTIENT $1.95

Mall bars can be lumped into two categories: inside and outside. Inside mall bars' raison d'etre is to serve the needs of the shoppers. Outside mall bars are legitimate destinations, and one of the best examples is Bravo in Waldorf's St. Charles Towne Center Mall.

It's a huge place (as mall bars go) with about a third of the floor space occupied by a high-tech semi-circular bar surrounded by glass, tile and neon. Above the bar hang three large monitors locked in on sports channels, and above the monitors hang about a hundred sports team pennants. So, the place is a sports bar. But the majority of the patrons don't come to see what's on the tube. They come to see what's on the "specials" list.

Each weekday at Bravo, there's a free entree with a complementary discounted beverage. Mondays, it's Italian sausage with Lowenbraus for a buck. Tuesday, the offering is slabs of six-foot sub accompanied by Long Island ice teas priced at $1.99, and the deals run through Friday, when the freebie du jour is steamship round of beef along with $1.99 margaritas.

But I haven't touched on what really sets the Waldorf Bravo (part of a small chain scattered throughout Maryland) apart from its other mall-inhabiting contemporaries. Behind the glitzy bar, there's a roaring fire, but it's not contained in a fireplace. Bravo has it's own Italian-made wood-burning oven which bakes up some mighty righteous pizzas, and slices of those pies are free during Thursday happy hours (there's also a $5.99 all-you-can-eat pizza deal on Sundays).

Both standard and strange toppings are offered on the Bravo pizzas. You can opt for the familiar (pepperoni, sausage, mushrooms) or you can yuppie it up with sauteed spinach, zucchini, eggplant and chicken.

For liquor drinks that don't taste like liquor, there's a nice selection of potent ice cream drinks at Bravo. And for those working on their beer belly, Miller & Miller Lite drafts go for 90 cents from four til 10 every Tuesday.

BEST TIME TO VISIT

Thursday and Friday happy hours are best bets, as well as their Sunday pizza feeding frenzy, when the first draft sells for a quarter.

HOURS: Mon.-Sat. 11-1; Sun. 11-12

HAPPY HOUR: Mon.-Fri. 4-7 discount drinks and free hot munchies

ENTERTAINMENT: Wed. karaoke

ACCEPTABLE PLASTIC: All but D

ISLAND INN

Main Street
Cobb Island, MD
(301) 259-2600

YUPPIE APPEAL 3
MUNCH FACTOR 1
COMFORT ZONE 2
BUD QUOTIENT $1.75

Perhaps you want to really get away from it all - get away from the city and its gotta-have-a-gimmick nightspots (although it's those gimmicks which differentiate one club from another). If so, take a drive down to Cobb Island.

Located 12 miles off of Rte. 301 in the deepest, most rural section of Charles County, Cobb Island is more for the back-to-basics crowd than the party-hearty segment. There, you'll find unspoiled shoreline to explore, working marinas to peruse, a few first-class seafood restaurants to enjoy and the Island Inn.

After dinner at one of those restaurants located at the entrance to the island, take a two-block walk inland and settle back at the Island Inn. During the summer, the place will be filled with both working watermen and recreational boaters, white collar and blue collar types, and maybe even a representative or a state senator or two.

If you happen to be there during a Redskin game (you're in hardcore Redskin territory), it would behoove you to root for the home team. It's Redskin shooters (the recipe varies monthly) on the house after each score.

If you happen to be there on a Wednesday evening, you might be coerced into entering an in-house, split-the-pot pool tournament. And local musician, Bill Mendez, takes the microphone on summer Sundays from seven until midnight.

Although the Island Inn is a basic rural waterfront bar with absolutely no pretensions, if you look hard, you'll see a few urban influences. Although only two domestic best selling brews are drawn on tap, between the Bud and Coors sticks is a tap for chablis and white zin. Hidden behind the Seagram's 7 and Jack Daniel's on the backbar is a full contingent of Absolut vodkas (80- and 100-proof, Citron and Peppar). And you can get an Amstel there without getting a puzzled look from the bartender.

Pub food at the Island Inn is the norm: burgers, onion rings and pizza, but this is seafood-eating country with the nearby restaurants getting the nod when it comes to cuisine.

HOURS: Mon.-Sun. 6a.m.-2

HAPPY HOUR: Mon.-Fri. 3-5 discount rail drinks and 50-cent drafts

ENTERTAINMENT: Sun. one-man acoustic and karaoke in summer

ACCEPTABLE PLASTIC: None

BEST TIME TO VISIT

Come by Sundays during the early evening for the music and the crowd.

McCAULEY'S PUB

Highway 925
Waldorf, MD
(301) 645-7709

YUPPIE APPEAL 1
MUNCH FACTOR 1
COMFORT ZONE 2
BUD QUOTIENT $2.00

What was old Waldorf like before Washington encroached and made it the latest metropolitan suburb? It was like McCauley's Pub still is.

It wasn't that long ago when you could escape D.C. and head for the country in nearby northern Charles County. But now, Waldorf has its own yuppie enclave, St. Charles Village (Columbia South), the major shopping center (I'm sorry, "shopping centre") contains a yuppie pizza emporium, Bravo's (featured herein), and the latest link in a chain of upscale food & drink establishments, Ruby Tuesday.

In the midst of all this urban influence, there's McCauley's Pub. Located just off the main Waldorf drag (Rte. 301), McCauley's is a deceptively large tavern. It's front room is an inviting, dimly lit saloon with a brickfront bar facing a backbar containing a huge variety of liquors four levels high. Casablanca fans spin lazily above and a woodburning fireplace in the corner is fired up when the temperature outside drops.

Beyond the saloon is a large game room filled with six well-maintained and well-spaced pool tables and about a dozen video games and pinball machines. There's also a dart room off of the main barroom.

It seems the 20-year-old pub hasn't forgotten its roots. While other happy hour patrons in other Waldorf bars are sipping three dollar imports, McCauley's customers enjoy 65-cent Buds and 75-cent Killians. For those who want something a little fancier, there are a few bottled imports available including Harp and Guinness Stout (after all, this is an Irish pub).

Food at McCauley's doesn't get much more elaborate than half smokes and subs, but it's good grub at McDonald's prices.

So, to recap, you can go elsewhere in Waldorf and have a pitcher of Bass Ale, or you can go to McCauley's and have a couple pitchers of Bud and a half smoke, play a few racks of eight ball, and play a few games of shuffleboard bowling for the same price.

BEST TIME TO VISIT

Every month or so, McCauley's brings in a rock or top-40 band, and the joint rocks until two. Call for the next scheduled live appearance.

HOURS: Mon.-Sat. 11-2; Sun. 12-12

HAPPY HOUR: Mon.-Fri. 4-7 65-cent Bud draft, $3.25 pitchers

ENTERTAINMENT: Monthly rock or top-40 bands

ACCEPTABLE PLASTIC: None

RIVERBOAT

301 Beach Terrace
Colonial Beach, VA
(804) 224-7055

YUPPIE APPEAL	3
MUNCH FACTOR	3
COMFORT ZONE	3
BUD QUOTIENT	$2.00

And now for a short history lesson. In 1623, King Charles I bestowed Mary Land to Lord Baltimore, and because L.B. was the king's favorite, Charles threw in the entire Potomac river as part of the package. Today, Maryland still lays claim to the Potomac.

Twelve miles south of the Potomac River bridge which links the southern tip of Maryland's Charles County to the Northern Neck of Virginia sets the small Potomac River resort community of Colonial Beach. And set atop pilings above the river there is Riverboat on the Potomac - a Maryland (Charles County) club deep in the heart of Virginia.

You should have seen the place five years ago. Back then it was known as Little Reno and, being a Maryland establishment, it played host to tens of thousands of Virginia lottery players each week. Sales of Maryland Lottery tickets had made the place a goldmine until Virginia instituted its own lottery. After that, the place became just one more of the 100 area waterfront watering holes.

New owners have recently taken over the club on the Potomac, and plan to reinstate it to its former prominence.

Parachute silks will line the ceiling of the St. John room where live bands will crank out oldies and southern rock Thursdays through Saturdays. And on Sundays, the bands will take to the huge covered porch, comfortably seating 60 and complete with its own sit-down bar. Those wanting a temporary escape from the main throng can take a seat on the wraparound porch with a view of the Potomac (so wide at this point, the opposite shore is beyond the horizon), and the old Little Reno pier.

Although the entire restaurant menu will be made available in the lounge and on the porch, best bites will come from the large sandwich selection and raw bar offerings.

Most beer drinkers will find a brew to their liking at the Riverboat with three drafts and 20 different bottled brands on the menu, but the porch is definitely a place to stretch back and slip slowly on a rhumb runner, fresh strawberry daiquiri or mai-tai.

HOURS: Mon.-Sat. 8a.m.-2;
Sun. 8-12 (summer); 10-10 off-season

HAPPY HOUR: Mon.-Fri. 3-6 discount rail drinks and munchies

ENTERTAINMENT: Thurs.-Sun. live oldies, country or southern rock bands

ACCEPTABLE PLASTIC: V,MC,AE

BEST TIME TO VISIT

On June 12-14, Colonial Beach stages its Potomac River Festival, and all festivities (parades, exhibitions and fireworks) take place next to the Riverboat.

ROBERTSON'S CRAB HOUSE

Pope's Creek Road
Newburg, MD
(301) 934-9236

YUPPIE APPEAL 3
MUNCH FACTOR 4
COMFORT ZONE 3
BUD QUOTIENT $1.75

Setting on a corner of the bar inside Robertson's Crab House are two frozen drink machines, the type you normally find churning endlessly at soda shoppes. In one of those machines is a house creation called "Crab Cooler" and in the other is a red slushy concoction known as "Back Rub."

Even though Robertson's large bar boasts four drafts (all domestic) and a half dozen imports along with wines on tap and a complete liquor selection, just under three quarters of sales there are for Back Rubs, made with a variety of rums and a secret ingredient the proprietor refuses to divulge. He did, however, reveal that his popular house drink (served up in a brandy snifter) was a 45 percent alcohol (90-proof) refresher. Drink 'em carefully.

Robertson's, located directly on the Potomac (where it's width measures close to three miles) at Pope's Creek, may be situated in a non-resort area, but the site is far from being a non-tourist destination. Boaters and city dwellers flock to Pope's Creek in the summer for authentic Maryland seafood in an authentic waterfront setting. And all of that indigenous cuisine is offered at the bar and lounge section inside Robertson's.

The large oak bar there is an irregularly-shaped structure allowing patrons to either sit in the mainstream or retreat to a more secluded corner, and the adjoining lounge is filled with large tables and booths to accommodate the horde of steamed crab fans, who have been returning to the place for over a half century.

Meanwhile, back at the bar, patrons are sipping Back Rubs and sampling other items from the menu, from scallops to soft shells, and finishing up with a slab of Key Lime pie or an Irish Coffee.

Unlike many of the Southern Maryland seafood emporiums that like to tuck their bar patrons away in a small corner of their establishment, Robertson's large interior is split across the middle (half bar/lounge, half restaurant). Unfortunately, it's the restaurant patrons who gets those great waterfront window seats.

BEST TIME TO VISIT

On any Saturday evening in the summer, the bar and lounge is filled with boaters and urbanites escaping the city for the day. Get there before sunset.

HOURS: Mon.-Sat. 11-11; Sun. 11-9 (summer); call for off-season times

HAPPY HOUR: None

ENTERTAINMENT: Mixed music via jukebox

ACCEPTABLE PLASTIC: V,MC

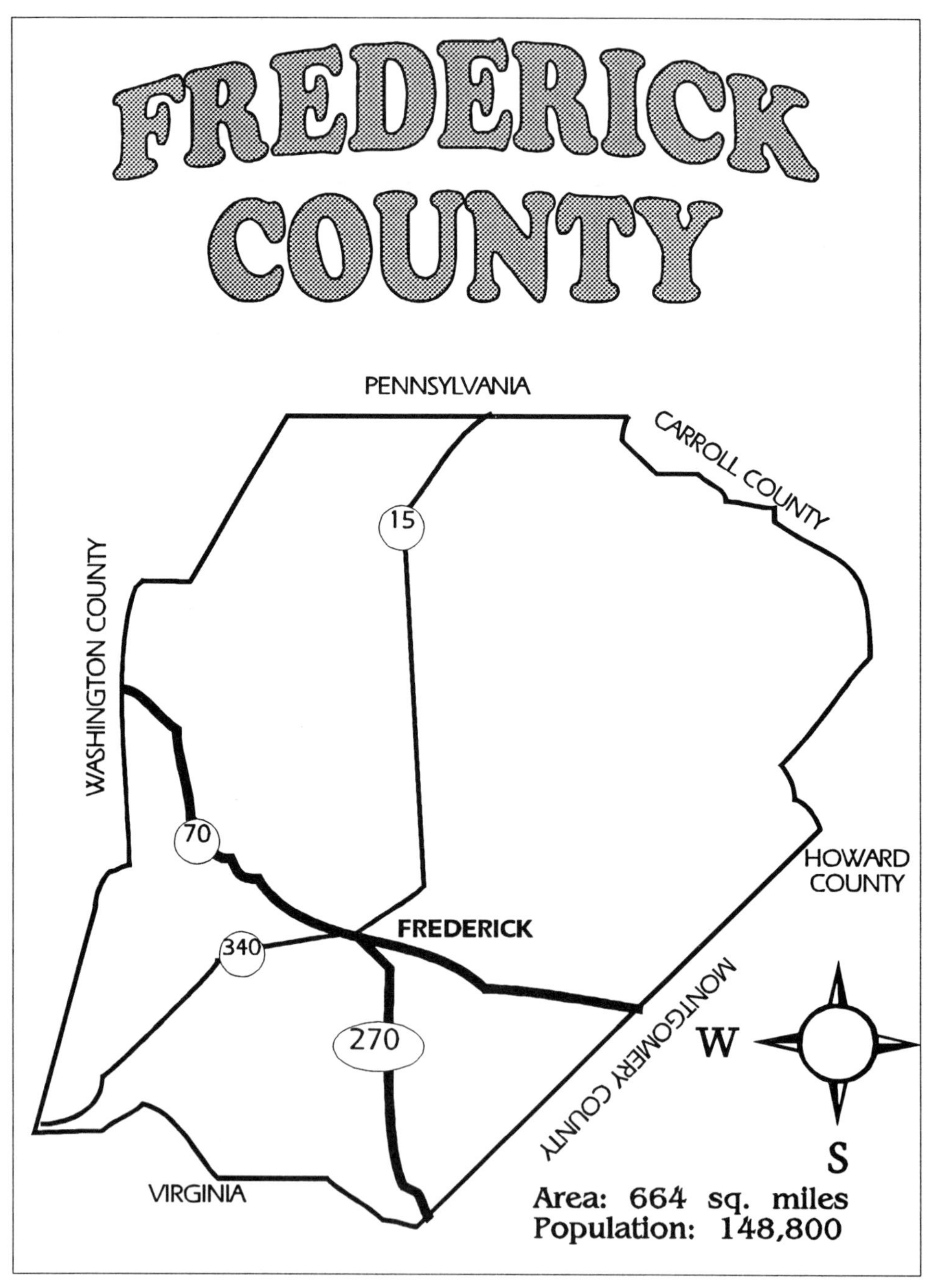
FREDERICK COUNTY
PENNSYLVANIA
CARROLL COUNTY
WASHINGTON COUNTY
15
70
FREDERICK
340
270
HOWARD COUNTY
MONTGOMERY COUNTY
VIRGINIA
W
S
Area: 664 sq. miles
Population: 148,800

THE BROWN PELICAN

5 E. Church Street
Frederick, MD
(301) 695-5833

YUPPIE APPEAL 5
MUNCH FACTOR 1
COMFORT ZONE 3
BUD QUOTIENT $2.00

In the most general sense, downtown Frederick taverns can be broken down into two major categories: those with live entertainment and those without. The next category breakdown is yuppie and non-yuppie. The Brown Pelican is a great example of a Frederick non-entertainment/yuppie establishment.

That non-entertainment classification is rather clear-cut, but what are its qualifications for yuppie status? Just take a look at the Pelican's food and drink listings. At all times, there are at least a half dozen wines offered by the glass. During a recent visit, those single-serve vintages included three Californians, two Chileans and one New Yorker. In addition, there's always a couple of sparklers-by-the-glass. And a surprisingly long wine list advertises dozens of selections from an $11 Napa Gewurztraminer to a $120 French burgundy.

The Brown Pelican's liquor collection reflects the taste of the 30-and-over white-collar patrons who inhabit the bar. There's a huge variety of single-malt and blended scotches next to eight rums and a full complement of the yuppie staple, Eurovodkas. Then, there's the menu.

How do these appetizers sound: lobster cocktail, wild mushrooms in puff pastry, marinated artichoke hearts, or shrimp remoulade? There's also pasta-for-two appetizer selections featuring fettucine and angel hair. This is not your average neighborhood pub grub.

Containing perhaps the smallest bar in downtown Frederick, the Brown Pelican's lounge is often filled on weekend nights by personnel from nearby food and beverage operations, and those taking a quiet respite from the nearby

entertainment/yuppie clubs.

Not every night is like the one before at the Brown Pelican. A sizable segment of the patrons there are drawn by the man or woman behind the bar. Surprisingly, Tuesdays, Thursdays and Sundays are shooter-intensive. And the mixologist behind the bar on Fridays and Saturdays specializes in the "Big Pour."

BEST TIME TO VISIT

Drop in on a Friday or Saturday after midnight for a nightcap, and ask the bartender if you (only if you're a woman, I think) can add you lip prints to the collection.

HOURS: Mon.-Fri. 11:30-2; Sat.-Sun. 5-2

HAPPY HOUR: 11:30 p.m.-1:30 a.m. two-for-one beer and rail drinks

ENTERTAINMENT: Eclectic mix of music via tapes

ACCEPTABLE PLASTIC: V,MC,AE

DONNELLY'S SALOON

103 N. Market Street
Frederick, MD
(301) 695-5388

YUPPIE APPEAL 5
MUNCH FACTOR 3
COMFORT ZONE 4
BUD QUOTIENT $2.38

This place has more atmosphere than any one place should have. Walk through its front door any afternoon and it's like walking through a time portal. I've always been a sucker for establishments like this; taverns that accurately recreate the bar where John Wayne shot it out in the last scene of *The Shootist*, taverns that recreate the "modern saloons" of the 1890's, taverns where the bare wooden floors creak beneath your feet as you saunter up to a big imposing bar. If they could just legally fulfil the request, "Gimme a whiskey and leave the bottle," this place would be perfect.

Behind the large mahogany-stained cherry serving bar are these two colossal antique Adams' fireplace mantles serving as the backbar. Twenty-five feet above the floor is an ornately decorated gold tin ceiling. And a second story loft offers diners and drinkers the best downtown seats in Frederick. Those loft window tables are always the first to fill.

Meanwhile, back at the bar, patrons are drinking decidedly un-western potables like Half & Halfs (six ounces of Guinness floating atop six ounces of Harp lager), Marcus James wines, and Absolut.

During Happy Hour, the price of steamed shrimp drops dramatically (from $6.95 to $2.95 for a half pound) and raw shellfish go for 60 cents apiece.

Skins and wings are served at the bar along with a wide array of sandwiches stuffed with everything from chicken to catfish, and there's a complete raw bar for those with a taste for things uncooked.

On Fridays and Saturdays after the sun goes down, Donnelly's does take on a bit of a wild west persona (well, *wild* anyway). Classic rock and progressive bands take to the stage, but as the night progresses, band members often take their act to the top of the bar (along with a customer or two).

High above the backbar is a huge portrait of Peter Donnelly, namesake of the bar, and a stuffed jackelope (a rabbit with antlers) which, the saloon owner swears (without cracking as much as a smirk), was shot by Peter in the 1800s.

There never were jackelopes, were there? My computer spellcheck never heard of it.

HOURS: Mon.-Sat. 11:30-2; Sun. 11:30-12

HAPPY HOUR: Mon.-Fri. 4:30-7 half-price drinks & shrimp

ENTERTAINMENT: Fri.-Sat. live progressive & classic rock

ACCEPTABLE PLASTIC: V,MC,AE

BEST TIME TO VISIT

To really appreciate the saloon, mosey up to the bar around three in the afternoon.

JENNIFER'S

207 W. Patrick Street
Frederick, MD
(301) 662-0373

YUPPIE APPEAL 4
MUNCH FACTOR 4
COMFORT ZONE 2
BUD QUOTIENT $2.25

It's hard to pigeonhole Jennifer's Restaurant. It could be called a neighborhood restaurant, but it's more than that. It could be called a neighborhood pub, but it's more than that, too.

Located in the first floor of a small 120-year-old home (whose previous claim to fame was as a 1920's brothel, I'm told) Jennifer's front room houses the bar, some well-spaced tables and a few hardwood booths. About 50 flags of countries, schools, breweries, etc. hang from the beamed ceiling. At the far end of the pub room is a large working fireplace, and at the left enveloping a bare brick wall, there's a combination bar and display area featuring the desserts and wines offered.

At that bar is a nice selection of brews with Bass and Anchor Steam on tap and 26 bottled beers including names you rarely see in small neighborhood taverns such as Old Peculiar, Pilsner Urquell and Fischer.

Even when the fireplace isn't roaring, Jennifer's dessert coffees are big sellers. Cambridge Coffee spiked with Frangelico, Irish cream with chocolate and whipped cream heads the list of the 10 mug drinks.

And the food served at the bar (and in the adjoining dining room) is not the stuff you normally see listed in small neighborhood taverns. Light fare there includes such tempting offerings as antipasto, quesadillas, Cajun chicken fingers with honey-Dijon mustard, mushrooms stuffed with crab & cheeses and a platter of fruits and cheeses.

Jennifer's pizzas are the Boboli-crusted variety that can be as traditional or as yuppified as you like. Their white pizza with garlic butter and mozzarella can turn into a Maryland pizza with the addition of some crabmeat and Old Bay. Non-carnivores will like the California rendition: sprouts, mushroom, onion and tomatoes.

Couples make up the bulk of the clientele at Jennifer's (the place is the antonym of "meat market"). It's a "Cheers" atmosphere where the music is not overwhelming and entertainment is the old-fashioned kind - conversation.

BEST TIME TO VISIT

In the winter when the fireplace is roaring, there not a more inviting haven from the cold.

HOURS: Tues.-Sat. 11:30-12; Sun.-Mon. 11:30-10

HAPPY HOUR: None

ENTERTAINMENT: Light jazz & blues via CD & tapes

ACCEPTABLE PLASTIC: V,MC,AE

LA TRATTORIA

6 East Street
Frederick, MD
(301) 663-6600

YUPPIE APPEAL	4
MUNCH FACTOR	5
COMFORT ZONE	4
BUD QUOTIENT	$1.95

Wouldn't it be great if there was just one tavern in Maryland that really treated pizza as a gourmet meal? I'm talking about a first class establishment serving up first class pizza accompanied by first class beverages. In a state full of Pizza Hut, Shakey's and Chuck E. Cheese outlets, It's nice to know there's a La Trattoria around when you want it.

Contained within the super slick Tauraso's Ristorante along Frederick's antique row, the casual pub called La Trattoria is the ultimate venue for pizza and wine. It just doesn't get any better than this.

There's plenty of room at the huge square bar to savor the pie and vino, plus there are plenty of window seats overlooking the quiet side of Frederick to drink and dine.

Over 25 wines from California and Europe's best vintners are available by the glass, but if you want to share a bottle of wine with your pie, your options become far more numerous. Over 280 brands and vintages (including 50 California chardonnays alone) are there.

You want beer with your pizza? No problem. La Trattoria boast a beer list containing over 50 entries including such great oddities as Belgian raspberry and cherry beers, and two featured "beer-of-the-day" microbrews.

Those pizzas, baked in a wood burning oven (by a chef and not some kid), are incredible lumpy, bumpy savory pies that can be topped with yuppie fixins like fresh goat cheese, pancetta (Italian bacon) and artichoke hearts, or the standard fare.

Dinners this good are meant to be topped off with a little something special. La Trattoria offers 19 brandies and cognacs starting at a very reasonable $3, and 15 sherries and ports averaging about $3.25. A cappuchino flavored with Vandermint is also a good choice. But if you've had enough to drink, there's always a dish of Bananas Foster (weight watchers beware) for two.

It should be mentioned that La Trattoria's pub menu contains 40 other entries other than the pizza, but (trust me) that pizza is worth driving hours to get to.

HOURS: Sun.-Thurs. 11-11; Fri.-Sat. 11-2

HAPPY HOUR: Mon.-Fri. 4:30-6 half-price drinks & cheese pizza

ENTERTAINMENT: Classical music on CD

ACCEPTABLE PLASTIC: All but D

BEST TIME TO VISIT

A basic cheese pizza and all drinks are half price during Happy Hour. Enough said.

McDONALD'S RAW BAR

6 S. Bentz Street
Frederick, MD
(301) 694-9134

YUPPIE APPEAL 2
MUNCH FACTOR 4
COMFORT ZONE 2
BUD QUOTIENT $1.50

You can drive right by the place and never know that you passed a tavern. You can look at the sign and not know what what's really going on inside. You can walk through the front door and still not know what the place is all about. McDonald's Raw bar is one of Frederick's best kept secrets.

McDonald's looks like a garage to passers-by. It had been a garage (actually, a radiator shop) for decades and the current owners have done little to change the exterior facade.

When you walk into McDonald's, you'll think your in a little ma & pa diner. There's a counter on the right lined with soda shoppe stools. There's a Wurlitzer on your left, and a few naugahyde upholstered booths hugging the opposite wall. Then you'll spot the beer signs, not the cheap plastic come-ons but rather the real neon jobs, around the top of the wall.

There's a doorway leading from the diner to the garage which is filled with brown paper covered picnic tables, more of those great neon signs, and a stage.

McDonald's has quietly become central Maryland's foremost rhythm & blues bar regularly hosting such names as Deanna Bogart, The Nighthawks and the infamous Root Boy Slim. It's a no-nonsense nightclub for music, beer and crabs.

Twenty-five different brews, mostly the long-neck domestic variety, are the major beverages served both in the diner and garage/club. Fact is, McDonald's was the first bar in Maryland to offer its patrons a Bucket of Rocks (six Rolling Rocks in an ice filled bucket).

Cuisine there is as simple as a bushel of Chesapeake blues or an oyster shooter (shot glass filled with a fresh shucked oyster, Japanese horseradish, tabasco, Old Bay, pepper and beer for $1.50), or as elegant as eight sushi selections ($10.95) or a main lobster.

McDonald's raw bar features mussels, oysters, clams, spiced shrimp and crab legs, and a wide variety of seafood sandwiches (including softshell) are available.

When construction on the Carroll Creek finishes in two years, McDonald's patio seats will become some of the most coveted real estate in Frederick County.

BEST TIME TO VISIT

Friday Happy Hours are a good bet. Then stay for the show.

HOURS: Mon.-Sat. 11-2; Sun. 1-2

HAPPY HOUR: Mon.-Fri. 4-6 discount beer & munchies

ENTERTAINMENT: Fri.-Sun (summer); Thurs.-Sat. (winter) live rhythm & blues

ACCEPTABLE PLASTIC: V,MC,AE

WAG'S

24 S. Market Street
Frederick, MD
(301) 694-8451

YUPPIE APPEAL 1
MUNCH FACTOR 4
COMFORT ZONE 3
BUD QUOTIENT $1.66

Market Street, Frederick: A dozen first-class watering holes lined along an eight-block stretch. The perfect starting block for a Market Street pub crawl is at the southern end of the strip at a place called Wag's.

Wag's is small, classic basement bistro specializing in ABCD (alcohol beverages, conversation and dining). Although nothing like the status-conscious pubs you'll encounter along your Market Street crawl, Wag's is nonetheless a classy and comfortable establishment featuring a long solid oak frontbar and backbar across from a line of candlelit tables. Framed ads from turn-of-the century newspaper, and old tintypes run along the walls of the narrow, dimly lit bar that terminates at a single dart board.

Nearly every establishment that serves food boasts fresh food, but at Wag's you can be sure that the food's fresh - THE KITCHEN DOESN'T HAVE A FREEZER! The meats and vegetables that go into Wag's tavern fare arrive fresh daily. Don't look for the traditional finger fare such as fried cheese sticks, chicken fingers or similar freezer-to-fryer foods. Look for the Wagburger topped with provolone, onions and a special house sauce. Look for Wag's fries: fresh cut Idaho potatoes twice-cooked in peanut oil. And look for Wag's Phiily cheese steak made from fresh-sliced top round. The most recent kitchen addition is a hickory smoker turning out authentic pit beef (brisket) with Wag's signature sauce on a kaiser roll.

Ten imports and ten domestic brews are there to accompany the burgers and all. The wines of Sangre de Toro and Blossom Hill are served up by the glass. And if your choice is rum & Coke, ask for a Wag's rum & Coke (shaken, not stirred with lime juice). That backbar also holds a commendable variety of spirits including nine vodkas (mostly imports, off course), five gins and eight different brands of bourbon.

According to the owner, Wag's is not the place to prove your worth by jingling your BMW keys in front of the person sitting next to you (check out the *Yuppie Appeal* score).

HOURS: Mon.-Sat. 11-2; closed Sun.

HAPPY HOUR: Mon.-Fri. 4-7 two-for-one rail drinks & discount beer

ENTERTAINMENT: Eclectic mix (no rap) via tapes

ACCEPTABLE PLASTIC: None

BEST TIME TO VISIT

Start your Market Street pub crawl at six. Fill up on some good food, have a couple Happy Hour libations (2-for-1), and head north.

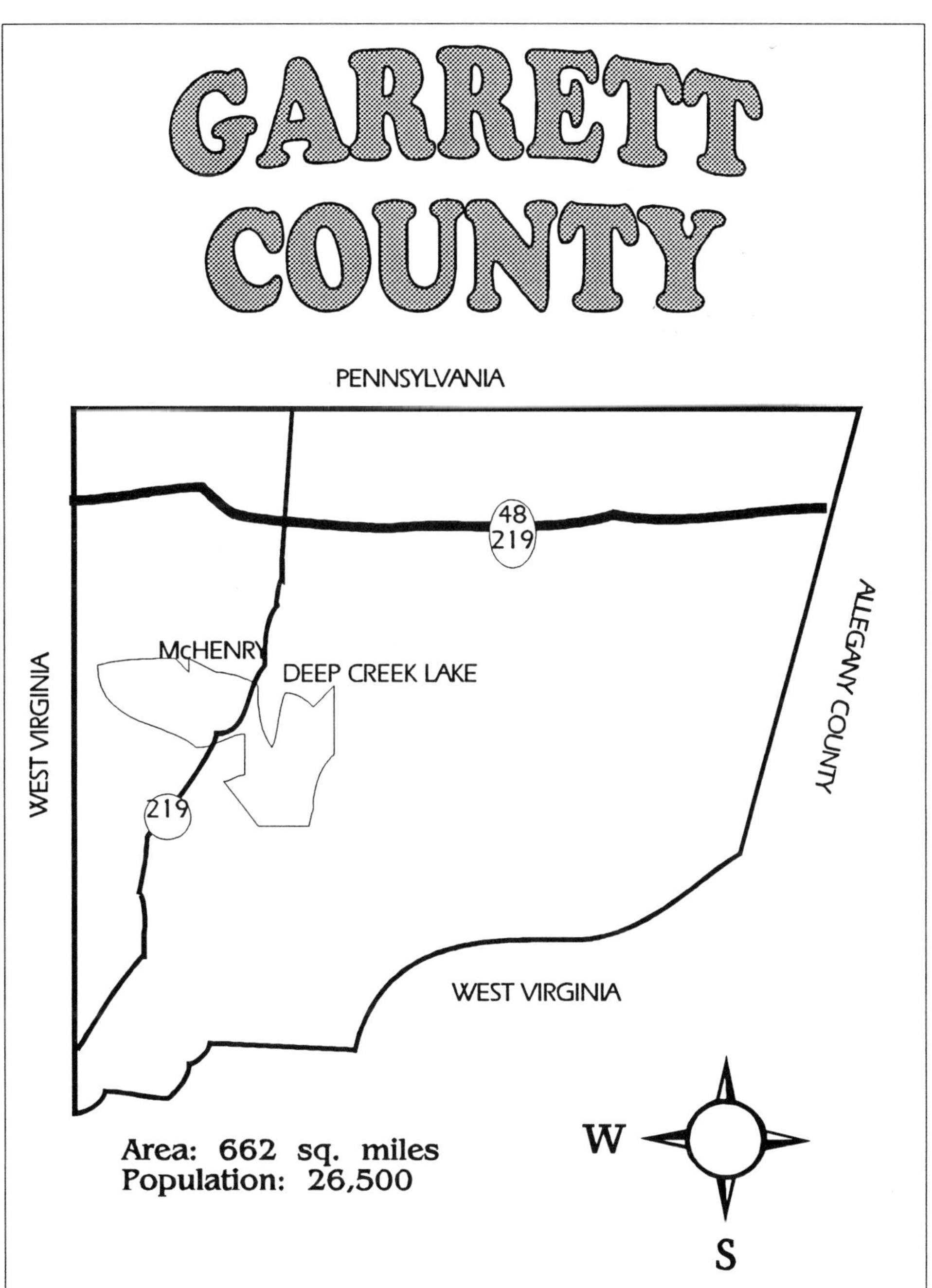
GARRETT COUNTY
PENNSYLVANIA
48
219
WEST VIRGINIA
McHENRY
DEEP CREEK LAKE
ALLEGANY COUNTY
219
WEST VIRGINIA
Area: 662 sq. miles
Population: 26,500
W
S

HONI-HONI

Rte. 219
Deep Creek Lake, MD
(301) 387-4866

YUPPIE APPEAL 3
MUNCH FACTOR 4
COMFORT ZONE 3
BUD QUOTIENT $1.90

You'll never hear *Moanie Moanie* sung by any of the bands playing at the Honi-Honi (a clause in their contracts prohibits that particular song). It's just not that kind of bar. The Honi-Honi's target audience during the summer (like that of The Harbor) is Yuppies...With Children.

You will hear country rock, oldies, top-40, and (on special occasions) even a little reggae if you get there early enough. During summer Saturdays, it's not unusual to see a half-mile string of cars parked along Rte. 219 during a Honi-Honi afternoon concert.

While children play on the large lawn leading down to the lakeshore, parents are imbibing one of Honi-Honi's eight special-recipe Tahitian concoctions topped with either shredded coconut or a drizzle of Myers' dark rum.

The corporation that owns the Deep Creek Lake Pizzeria Uno's (the area's most chic eatery) and the Arrowhead (the area's biggest grocery store) purchased and enlarged the Honi-Honi in 1989. All three enterprises share the same parking lot (the area's busiest).

With it's interior made solely of wood stripped from derelict ships and a bar which the management states is worth in excess of $20,000, the Honi-Honi strives hard to be like no other bar in Maryland's westernmost resort town.

Imbedded in 100 coats of polyurethane on the top of the Honi-Honi bar are shells and ship's ropes and a dozen solid gold Spanish doubloons dating back to the late 1700s. At the center of the backbar there's a shark jaw with a brass marker beneath it that reads "Caught in Deep Creek Lake in 1922." Deep Creek Lake was built (Maryland has no natural lakes) in 1925.

The entire menu from the adjacent Pizzeria Uno is available both at the Honi-Honi bar and its large patio which overlooks the widest portion of the lake, and during Happy Hour, raffles are held for deep discounts on deep dish pizzas and Honi-Honi attire (which have become some of the most coveted souvenirs in Deep Creek Lake).

HOURS: Mon.-Sun. 12-12 (summer); Fri.-Sun. most other days (call)

HAPPY HOUR: Mon.-Fri. 4-6 discount food coupons & Honi apparel raffles

ENTERTAINMENT: Live country, light rock, reggae or oldies

ACCEPTABLE PLASTIC: All but DC

BEST TIME TO VISIT

To best enjoy the food, the drinks and the view, visit the place in the off-season (before Memorial Day and after Labor Day). The Honi-Honi is open most weekends throughout the year.

SHENANIGAN'S

Wisp Ski Resort
McHenry, MD
(301) 387-4911

YUPPIE APPEAL 5
MUNCH FACTOR 1
COMFORT ZONE 3
BUD QUOTIENT $2.25

It doesn't matter whether you raced down Odin's Chute or slid sideways down Bellyflop Hill, when you've finished up at the Wisp slopes it's time to hit Shenanigan's.

Maryland's only major ski resort (there's a couple skiable hills in Frederick and Washington Counties), Wisp's beverage prices are nearly half those at nearby Virginia and West Virginia commercial slopes. California varietals there go for $2 a glass. Over 30 beers, including seven drafts and a dozen imports sell for the same price as a brew in town. But this is winter. You need a little anti-freeze, and Shenanigan's (along with its sister tavern, The 23 Degrees Below lounge) is the place to go. There's generous doses of Kahlua and Haagen-Dazs cream liqueur in steaming black coffee (Snowball), equally generous pours of spiced rum and coconut liqueur added to a mugs of hot chocolate (Hot Brownie), Heated Amaretto topped with a large dollop of whipped cream (Amaretto Hesse), plus a dozen other inside warmers. And every winter, Shenanigan's features two beverages known for their temperature-raising effects and sells them for $2. During the 1991-92 ski season, the featured warmers were Kirschwasser and Rumple Minze.

The bar also features 10 different Scotches, apparently the skier's favorite liquor category, and all of the high-dollar liqueurs from Amaretto to Yukon Jack.

The centerpiece of Shenanigan's lounge is a massive two-sided fireplace, and a nearby table is the perfect apres-ski site to sit back with a spiked coffee and an order of French fried provolone ($3.25).

Appetizers, averaging $3 each, are available at the bar, and in the pizzeria

next door, fresh dough pizzas bear prices starting at $5.95 and skyrocketing to $17.95 for a large Sicilian pie with the works.

Although known primarily as a winter destination, Wisp is a four-season resort with a championship golf course (rated the third most difficult in the state), hiking trails and an Olympic-size pool. But during the winter, there's no place in Maryland like it.

BEST TIME TO VISIT

Stop by Shenanigan's (you don't **have** to ski first) on a weekday during the winter for the best chance at a fireside seat.

HOURS: Mon.-Sun. 11-2 (during ski season)

HAPPY HOUR: None

ENTERTAINMENT: Jukebox and big screen TV

ACCEPTABLE PLASTIC: V, MC, D

SILVER TREE HARBOR

Glendale Road
Deep Creek Lake, MD
(301) 387-5524

YUPPIE APPEAL 3
MUNCH FACTOR 3
COMFORT ZONE 3
BUD QUOTIENT $1.75

It has the most inviting lounge of any of the Deep Creek Lake watering holes. The Tiffany Room inside the Silver Tree has perhaps the grandest backbar in the west, an intricately carved walnut creation totally framed with backlit stained glass that once graced a local barber shop. Adjacent to the bar are dozens of upholstered love seats and lounge chairs surrounding the Lake's biggest woodburning fireplace - a perfect winter sanctuary. That said, the best time to make your way to the Silver Tree is when the mercury is nearing the three-digit mark.

Nestled along the shores of Deep Creek's main lake is The Harbor, Silver Tree's summer escape. The lakeside pub, located just behind the main restaurant, was designed to accommodate the family trade (Deep Creek's bread and butter) during the afternoon and early evening, and the adult crowd at night. While mom and dad settle back of the large deck, their offspring are busy in the video game room or watching a Laurel & Hardy movie on The Harbor's new outdoor projection screen.

Most of the beer at The Harbor is the keg variety. A dozen taps dispense 10 different domestics. The popular imports are available in bottles. And fifteen varieties of frozen drinks are available along with a dozen different tooter shooters, including the house special Harbor-Harbor, a potent mixture of Amaretto, tequila, triple sec, Jack Daniels and Southern Comfort.

Cuisine at The Harbor includes half-pound burgers, chili dogs and chicken sandwiches, but the deck is a much more suitable venue for a bushel of steamed crabs, a platter of snow crab legs or a couple dozen shellfish from the adjoining raw bar. The Harbor is also one of the few waterfront establishments at the lake which serve up Baltimore staples like crab cakes and soft shells.

Originally built as a hunting lodge in the mid-1940s, the Silver Tree was converted into a restaurant/lounge in 1974 after two years of renovation, and it has remained one of the resort area's top draws year after year.

BEST TIME TO VISIT

With kids: from noon until six any summer day. Without kids: after nine any summer day, or after nine on a cold winter's night in the Tiffany Room.

HOURS: Mon.-Sat. 12-12; Sun. 12-6 (summer)

HAPPY HOUR: None

ENTERTAINMENT: Wed.-Sat. live top-40 bands

ACCEPTABLE PLASTIC: All

STRAY CAT CAFE

Old Deep Creek Drive
McHenry, MD
(301) 387-7440

YUPPIE APPEAL 3
MUNCH FACTOR 4
COMFORT ZONE 2
BUD QUOTIENT $1.75

The residents of Deep Creek Lake neighborhoods are lucky to have a neighborhood bar like this one. The owners of the Stray Cat Cafe have created a classic cantina with a little something for everyone.

Beneath the small restaurant is a series of rooms with more nooks and crannies than an English muffin. First, there's a game room filled with videos, air hockey and basketball. Turn a few corners and walk down a ramp to the cantina proper with its zig-zag bar and views of the lake. Turn another corner and walk up a few steps to the pool room.

The entire interior of the Stray Cat is created from pine and the walls are decorated with a clutter of authentic Americana and South-of-the-Border artifacts.

Fifteen beers (including the best three Mexican entries) are available (singly or in buckets of six) at the bar. You can get Western Maryland's finest margarita (original, peach, coconut or strawberry) there, which happens to share the number one request honors with a drink called a Red Snapper (Crown Royal & cranberry juice with a little Absolut).

Although the kitchen creates first-class burgers featuring a choice of 15 different toppings, and a host of hot finger foods with eight different dips, the biggest surprises are in the foreign fare.

Instead of the homogenized cookie-cutter cuisine found in the Mexican food chains, the Stray Cat menu has an entire page (big page) devoted to the made-to-order foods that were meant to be washed down with a Carta Blanca or two; quesadillas, chicken and beef based nachos, and single servings from the entire line of Tex-Mex offerings from burritos to tostados.

Although the food and drink and decor of the Stray Cat Cafe are nothing less than first rate, the place doesn't take itself all that seriously. Last April Fools Day, the owner brought in a donkey for "Have a Drink with a Total Ass Day." And newcomers are often offered a free house drink called a Cement Mixer (even if you don't believe anything else that I've written in this book, believe this - *don't drink the Cement Mixer*).

BEST TIME TO VISIT

To get the best idea of what the place is all about, go there on "Tijuana Wing" day (Wednesday) around six.

HOURS: Mon.-Sat. 4-2

HAPPY HOUR: None

ENTERTAINMENT: Rock & blues in jukebox

ACCEPTABLE PLASTIC: V,MC

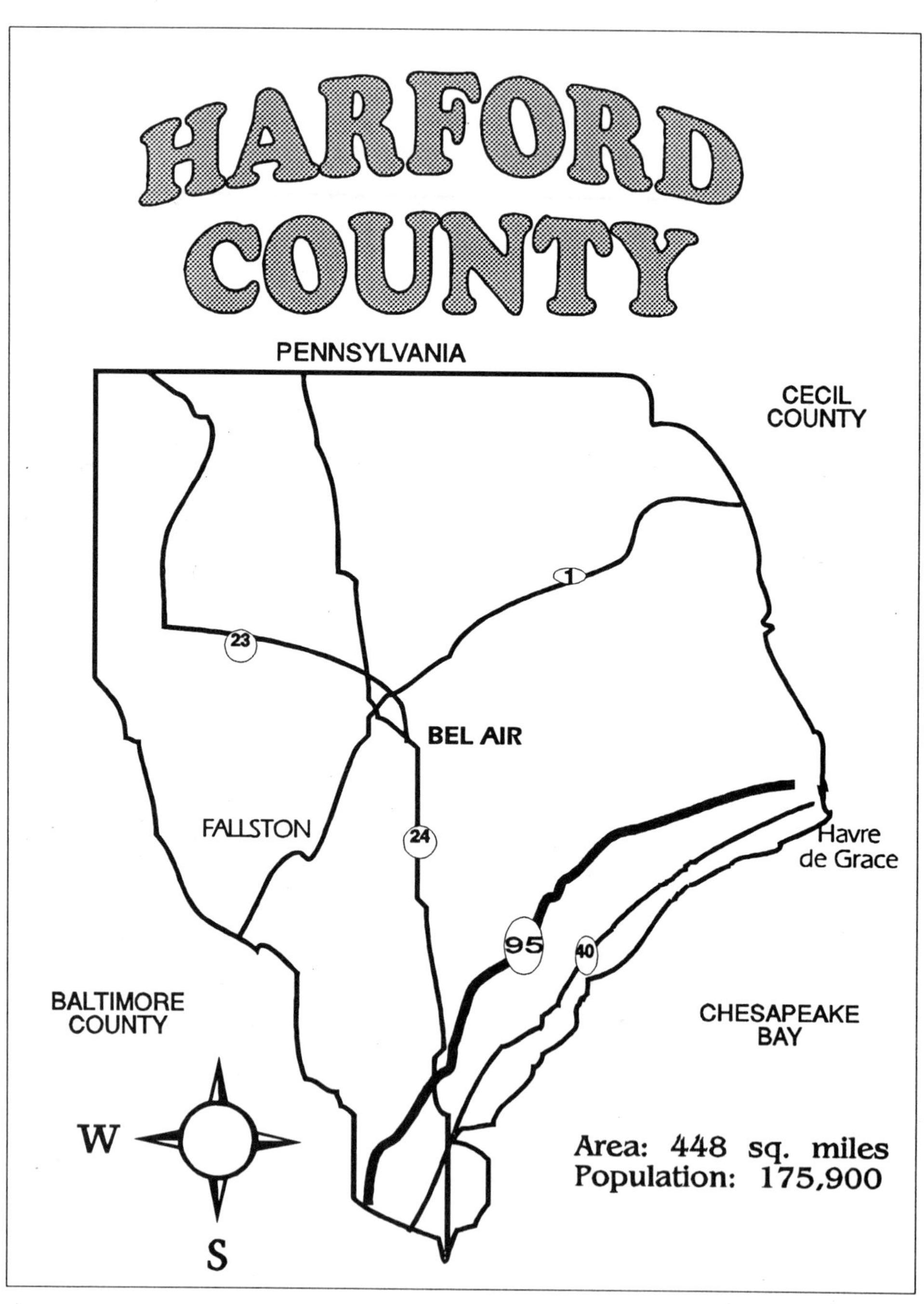
HARFORD COUNTY
PENNSYLVANIA
CECIL COUNTY
1
23
BEL AIR
FALLSTON
24
Havre de Grace
95
40
BALTIMORE COUNTY
CHESAPEAKE BAY
W
S
Area: 448 sq. miles
Population: 175,900

GEORGETOWN NORTH

12 S. Main Street
Belair, MD
(410) 879-0007

YUPPIE APPEAL 5
MUNCH FACTOR 3
COMFORT ZONE 3
BUD QUOTIENT $2.25

You'd expect to find a place like this in Annapolis or Fells Point...or Georgetown, so the name does fit. When the current owners took over the premises 12 years ago, they transformed the former rundown redneck dive into a classic urban retreat. When one Belair resident got his first look at the new place, he told the owner that it reminded him of a typical Georgetown tavern - and the name was born.

Nestled inside the first floor of a townhouse in one of the more historic sections of Harford County's capital city (they have a restaurant upstairs), Georgetown North's tavern has all of the interior fixings of its namesake's establishments. There's an exposed brick wall, plenty of bare hardwood below, and Casablanca fans, Tiffany-style lamps and track lights above.

Seventeen beers from the bottle, and five draft selections, including Sam Adams, Killian's and a surprising find - Dortmunder Dark, are available from the long, dark wood bar. Wines, other than the standards, get plenty of exposure. At any one time, 10 different wines by the glass (from a list that changes weekly) are offered.

If coffee drinks are your thing, they've got eight varieties, the most popular entry being Brazilian: Grand Marnier, Kahlua and brandy, topped with whipped cream sprinkled with nutmeg.

Food served either at the bar or in the adjacent room is definitely the upscale variety. There's a quiche du jour (how Georgetown can you get?), burgers all different ways (how about one with guacamole, bacon and hot pepper cheese?), and there are such things as a croissant club, Marco Polo and (attention rabbit food aficionados) a little something

called a Powerhouse: alfalfa sprouts, lettuce, muenster, etc. on seven grain toast.

Although Georgetown North serves mostly as a locals hangout during the week, catering to the white collar crowd from Happy Hour to closing, the tavern, on the weekend, become a destination for Baltimoreans, Delawareans, and nightlifers from as far away as Silver Spring and Frederick.

BEST TIME TO VISIT

Try to make it there on a Monday to meet their two best bartenders, and to get the true flavor of the place.

HOURS: Mon.-Sat. 11-2; Sun. 10-2

HAPPY HOUR: Mon.-Fri. 4-7; Sat. 11-6 50 cents off all drinks

ENTERTAINMENT: Mix of music via tapes

ACCEPTABLE PLASTIC: All

HUMMERS

2607 Belair Road
Fallston, MD
(410) 893-2034

YUPPIE APPEAL	3
MUNCH FACTOR	3
COMFORT ZONE	3
BUD QUOTIENT	$1.75

There's always something happening at Hummers. I guess when you have a nightclub in a small town like Fallston, you just have to try harder.

It's a big old club along Rte. 1 with a large two-tier lounge at one end and a sizable oval bar at the other, along with a stage and a couple assorted video games.

For reasons not readily apparent, Thursdays are the busiest nights at Hummers. I guess it could have something to do with the Thursday pricing structure at the bar - all rail drinks sell for a buck and a quarter.

But there's a special going on every night during the week. If there's a sport (any sport) being played on the tube on Monday nights, Hummers serves up beers for a buck and gives deep discounts at the raw bar. On Tuesdays, everything at the bar receives a discount (though not as high as Thursday).

Not much drinking goes on inside Hummers on Wednesday and Sunday nights. That's when the place sponsors a DJ spinning C\W discs, and gives its patrons (who'd rather dance than drink) free country dance lessons.

And it's rock & roll on Friday and Saturday featuring a live band, a DJ, or both.

It's probably safe to say that no other Fallston nightclub feeds its patrons as well as Hummers. You can wait until Friday happy hour there and load up on free goodies such as steamed shrimp or homemade sausage & peppers, or you can order from a mammoth selection of light fare produced fresh in the kitchen featuring three dozen sandwiches (half-pound burgers, crab melts, and on and on) plus 20 finger foods ranging in complexity from Buffalo wings to baked brie topped with sauteed apples and walnuts, which is a steal at $4.95.

House wines by the glass go for a respectable $2.25, and the bar offers a full selection of the hard stuff but, sadly, only one draft, Coors light, comes from a keg.

HOURS: Mon.-Sun. 11-2

HAPPY HOUR: Thurs.-Fri. 4-7
free hot buffet

ENTERTAINMENT: Fri.-Sat. live rock;
DJ & country dancing other nights

ACCEPTABLE PLASTIC: All but CB

BEST TIME TO VISIT

Take advantage of the free Friday night Happy Hour grub, then grab a good seat for the band. Then again, if country/western stomping is what you crave, head there on Sunday or Wednesday around 7.

MACGREGOR'S

331 St. John Street
Havre de Grace, MD
(410) 939-3003 (Balt.) 575-6910

YUPPIE APPEAL 3
MUNCH FACTOR 3
COMFORT ZONE 4
BUD QUOTIENT $2.25

If the dormant fireplace in MacGregor's Tavern were activated, the place would be just about perfect. But even as it is, MacGregor's is a grand spot to sit back and have a Bud and a burger. Wooden planking runs half way up the walls which are finished with a Williamsburg-type wallpaper, while ornaments are mostly pewter. And overhead are tiffany swag lamps and Casablanca fans. Plenty of seating is available at the oak bar and at numerous, well-spaced cafe tables.

The restaurant/tavern tucked away in the small Harford County waterfront community inhabits the old Havre de Grace Banking & Trust Company building, and a small alcove in the tavern occupies the space once used for the bank's vault.

Two domestics are available on draft, as well as Foster's and Killian's (yes, Killian's is made by Coors, but it's a step up from most commercial U.S. lagers), plus over two dozen bottled brands are there. And a full complement of spirits and liqueurs line the backbar.

MacGregor's "Lite Fare" menu is pretty awesome for pub grub. Sixteen different sandwiches are filled with such edibles as New York strip, lump crab cake and blackened chicken breast. And there are other savory offerings including smoked salmon and scallops wrapped in bacon. Plus, a seafood pizza created atop a Bobboli is smothered with whole steamed shrimp, whole scallops, and large chunks of backfin blue crab.

After the weather warms up, the action at MacGregor's moves from their great tavern to the 70-seat covered deck and gazebo overlooking the Susquehanna. Musicians, playing either country or contemporary sounds, work the deck until

8:30 on Fridays and 9:30 on Saturdays from mid-May through October.

Each month, MacGregor's promotes a new beer or mixed drink by selling it at a highly discounted price. And all restaurant specials (such as the $9.95 king-cut prime rib dinner on Mondays) carry over to the tavern where all waitresses are trained servers.

BEST TIME TO VISIT

On Fridays, MacGregor's serves up a free hot buffet featuring such goodies as Swedish meatballs and hot Italian sausages, and the later action on the gazebo is mostly singles oriented.

HOURS: Mon.-Sun. 11-2

HAPPY HOUR: Mon.-Fri. 3-7 two-for-one beer and rail; Fri. free buffet

ENTERTAINMENT: Fri.-Sat. live acoustic country or modern

ACCEPTABLE PLASTIC: All but D

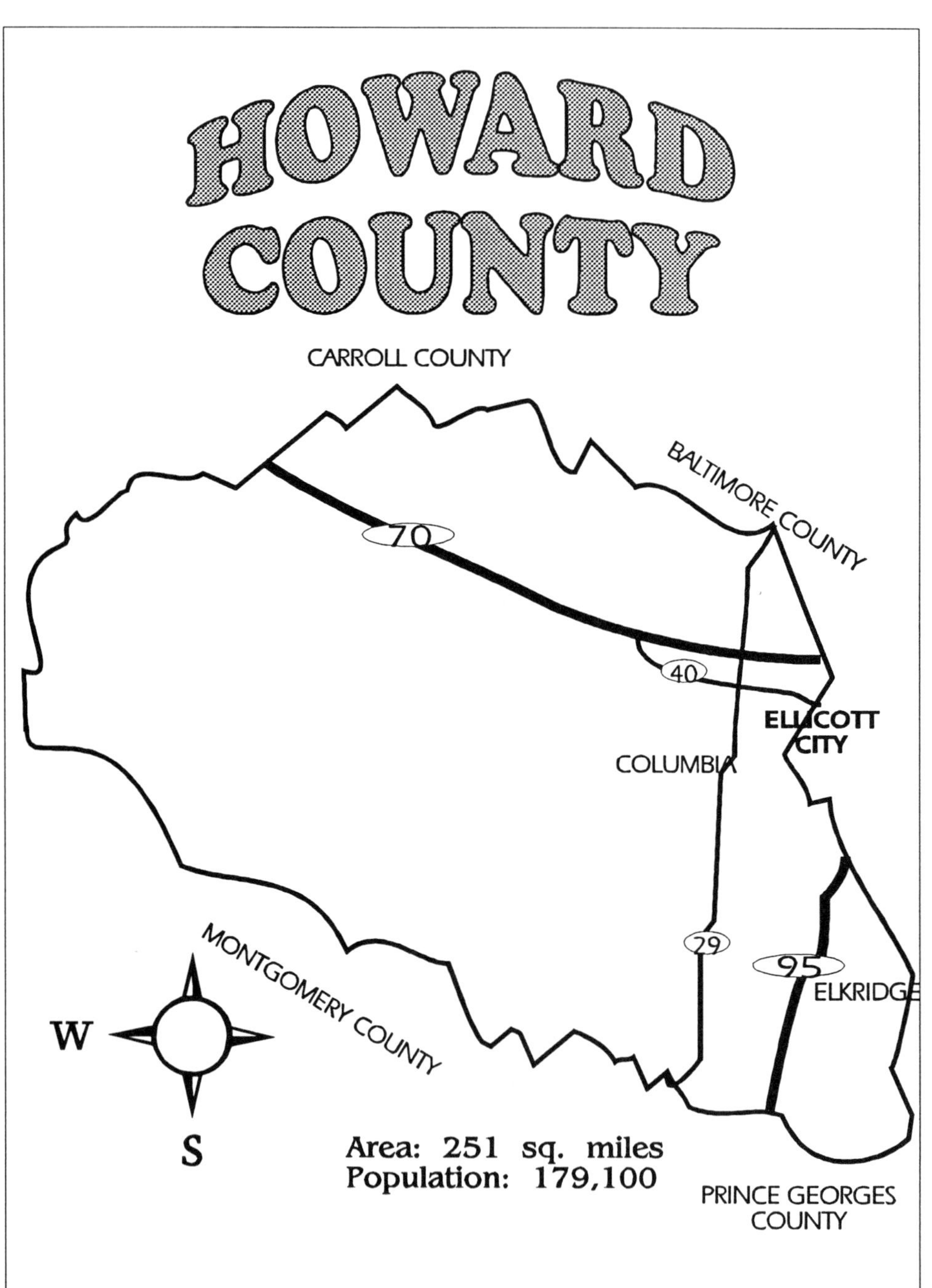
HOWARD
COUNTY
CARROLL COUNTY
BALTIMORE COUNTY
70
40
ELLICOTT
CITY
COLUMBIA
29
95
ELKRIDGE
MONTGOMERY COUNTY
W
S
Area: 251 sq. miles
Population: 179,100
PRINCE GEORGES
COUNTY

CACAO LANE

8066 Main Street
Ellicott City, MD
(410) 461-1378

YUPPIE APPEAL 4
MUNCH FACTOR 4
COMFORT ZONE 3
BUD QUOTIENT $1.90

You're surrounded by stone and hardwood in Cacao Lane, Ellicott City's most "atmospheric" food & beverage address, and the ultimate venue for a hot mulled cider on a December evening.

Most of the beers inside that granite edifice are the import and boutique variety (Wild Goose, Lightship, Rattlesnake, etc.) Cacao's wine selection, which changes weekly, reflects some of the best vintages that California has to offer (a recent selection included wines from the houses of Beaulieu, Kenwood and Huntington). Spirits displayed along the two antique buffets serving as the backbar are mostly from the high-dollar category, yet a snifter of Martell Cordon Rubie or a glass of premium armagnac is a respectable $4. And a mug of Cacao Lane's original hot mulled cider (fortified with three rums and three brandies) sells for $2.50. It seems that the management there knows that after the Howard County yuppie makes the payments on his condo and Beemer, there's little left for the finer things at the bar.

Contained on the first floor of the middle building of three comprising the Cacao Lane complex, the main lounge is but the first stop in an evening-long stay there. Two cozy and classy dining rooms flank both sides of the lounge, with the coziest and classiest tables-for-two next to the recessed windows facing the main lane. They're the best seats in Ellicott City and can be snagged only by reservation (call early).

After dinner (they've got a wonderful bouillabaisse and a "Baltimore's Best" Caesar salad along with a great selection of American and Continental selections), it's time to head upstairs to a slightly less formal lounge for some live jazz or rhythm & blues.

As this guide was going to press, Cacao Lane was just finishing its newest addition, an outdoor backyard terrace deck, which appears to be the perfect site to finish up the night with one of the establishment's 11 spiked international coffees such as the establishment's signature creation filled with creme de cacao, Baileys and Chambord.

BEST TIME TO VISIT

Catch the happy hour at the main lounge on a Friday around 5 before dinner. If you're a twosome, don't forget to reserve a window seat for dinner.

HOURS: Mon.-Sun. 11:30-2

HAPPY HOUR: Fri. 5-8 half-price burgers & dogs in the summer

ENTERTAINMENT: Fri.-Sat. live r&b, acoustic, jazz

ACCEPTABLE PLASTIC: V,MC,AE

DANIEL'S

5854 Washington Blvd.
Elkridge, MD
(410) 796-4678

Daniel's is a biker bar. Now, don't turn the page. Hear me out on this one.

There was a time, and not that long ago, when the phrase "Biker Bar" had negative connotations - real negative. But that was a time when all individuals who traveled on two wheels (most notably Harley Davidsons) were grouped by the public with a few bands of sociopathic morons bearing colorful names like "Pagans" and "Hell's Angels."

Today's biker (a person who travels via motorcycle) is usually a nine-to-fiver in a leather jacket (which provides a tad better protection from a spill than an Armani suit). And one of the bikers' favorite stopovers is Daniels - the restaurant with the bar on the outside.

When the weather warms, there's an unbroken string of chrome and steel parked in front of Daniels. The outdoor bar facing Rte. 1, along with the adjoining side deck, is filled with motorcyclists with one eye on their beer, the other on their bike. That bar on the outside of Daniels, which allows customers to keep tabs on their Harley, is a big reason why the place has been adopted by the two-wheel set. But it's not the only reason.

Instead of having his fish delivered by one of the dozen or so vendors from the Baltimore Fish Market (where 95 percent of Baltimore restaurants get their seafood), the owner of Daniels goes to that seafood warehouse himself and hand selects the entrees which will be served in his small restaurant (and at that outside bar).

For those who want traditional bar fare, Daniels has that in abundance including 20 different sandwiches (all made up fresh to order) ranging in price from a buck fifty to $3.50 for a fish filet or corned beef, and pizza.

But unfortunately, a large percentage of bargoers are going to miss out on the cuisine and the atmosphere at Daniels because the biker stigma remains.

Hey, they don't bite!

YUPPIE APPEAL 0
MUNCH FACTOR 3
COMFORT ZONE 1
BUD QUOTIENT $1.65

HOURS: Mon.-Sun. 7a.m.-2

HAPPY HOUR: None

ENTERTAINMENT: Rock via CD jukebox

ACCEPTABLE PLASTIC: MC

BEST TIME TO VISIT

On Oct. 15, bikers from all over Maryland participate in Motorcyclist's Operation Santa Claus. Over 3,000 toy-laden bikers head for Fort Smallwood park to deliver their gifts for area underprivileged children, and up to 1,500 motorcycles at any one time will be parked in and around Daniels.

LAST CHANCE SALOON

Oakland Mills Village Center
Columbia, MD
(410) 730-5656

YUPPIE APPEAL 4
MUNCH FACTOR 5
COMFORT ZONE 3
BUD QUOTIENT $1.79

I think it's safe to say that if I lived in Columbia, I would never have gotten this book finished by deadline. I would have been spending far too much time at the Last Chance Saloon. I love good beer, and that place is a beer lover's paradise.

The owner purchased $50,000 worth of beer dispensing equipment to have the beer flowing from the tap as cold as it was in its refrigerated keg. If $50,000 seems like an extraordinary sum just to transport beer from keg to glass, that's only because you don't know what an extraordinary tavern this is. The Last Chance Saloon is your basically traditional British pub - on steroids. The place offers 50 different draft beers! And only five of them are American mass-produced brews.

There, you'll find such wonderful pints as Schlosser Alt, Double Diamond, Anchor Porter, Franziscus, Murphy's Stout, Sam Adams Dopple Bock, and Spatan Dark (perhaps the finest single brew to ever land in Maryland).

The Last Chance's proprietor, an extremely knowledgeable beerophyle and only non-Brit to serve as judge at the prestigious Great Britain Beer Festival, gives three reasons why draft brews excel over their bottled and canned counterparts: "They're a better value," "They more closely resemble what the brewer intended," and "Bottles are an ecological disaster." And for those three reasons, you will rarely find a bottled beer in that saloon. And what a saloon.

Instead of the stereotypical yuppie pub decor (e.g. more ferns than in the Amazon tidal basin), the Last Chance's bar and adjacent large lounge is decorated with 250 beer bottles, 400 logoed beer coasters, and 200 English beer towels each advertising a different British brew. And in the 50-seat banquet room/dart parlor, 300 different domestic beer cans (many golden oldies) are on display.

Nearly two-dozen wines are offered by the glass there, and the pub food menu is one of the largest I've ever seen. Last Chance burgers are ambrosia.

Come to think of it, I shouldn't be telling you any of this. If too many people find out about this place, I'll have a hard time grabbing a good seat.

Just forget I ever mentioned the place.

BEST TIME TO VISIT
Go somewhere else!

HOURS: Mon.-Thurs. 11:30-1; Fri. 11:30-2; Sat. 4-2; closed Sun.

HAPPY HOUR: Tues.-Fri. discount beer, rail & house wine, munchies

ENTERTAINMENT: Fri.-Sat. live jazz, swing & boogey

ACCEPTABLE PLASTIC: V,MC,AE

PHOENIX EMPORIUM

8049 Main Street
Ellicott City, MD
(410) 465-5665

YUPPIE APPEAL 3
MUNCH FACTOR 3
COMFORT ZONE 2
BUD QUOTIENT $1.95

What does Minnie Pearl's hat and everything inside the Phoenix Emporium have in common? They all have a price tag.

When you first walk into the Phoenix, the first thing you'll notice will be the large glass-front refrigerator case behind the bar. Look inside and you'll see brews representing 22 different countries like Trinidad's Caribe, India's Kingfisher, Germany's Hofbrau and Scotland's McEwan's Ale. Collectively, you'll probably be looking at Howard County's biggest on-premise beer collections (plans are currently underway there to increase the number of brew labels past the 100-mark).

HOURS: Mon.-Sat. 11:30-2; Sun. 11-2

HAPPY HOUR: Mon.-Fri. 3:30-6:30 discount price on appetizers

ENTERTAINMENT: From hard rock to classics via tape

ACCEPTABLE PLASTIC: V,MC,AE

The second thing you'll notice is the abundance of "stuff" on the walls, on the various shelves and hanging from the ceiling. Look closer and you'll see that each piece of stuff has a price tag affixed to it. The Phoenix is Ellicott City's only beer, wine, liquor and antiques shoppe.

From a full spirit selection, the bartenders create 15 different potent coffees, teas and cocoas, plus a half dozen fresh fruit (in season) frozen jobs. Although the Phoenix offers an ever-changing wine list with a surprising selection of sparklers from a $14 Frexinet to a $95 Dom Perignon, most come here for the beer.

To go with those brews is a nice selection of finger foods (whose prices dip dramatically during Happy Hour) plus dozens of sandwich creations (including what they modestly describe as "The largest all-chuck burger in town"), salads and such. And while your sitting at the bar with you burger and Bass, you might want to haggle with the bartender over the antique oak backbar (asking price: $1,900). Antique kitchen gadgets, clocks, radios, brass registers, and a variety of old signs and stained glass hangings are also tagged. Want to buy the bar stool? Make an offer.

At least once a month, a huge promotion takes place at the Phoenix with the monster promo being "Jimmy Buffet Night," staged the Thursday night before Buffet's Merriweather concert featuring the food and drink of the Florida Keys, plus Buffet ballads all day long.

BEST TIME TO VISIT

The Phoenix flies on Fridays. Get there before eight if you want to enjoy the place from a seated position.

SNEAKERS SPORTS SALOON

8775 Cloudleap Court
Columbia, MD
(410) 730-2208

YUPPIE APPEAL 3
MUNCH FACTOR 3
COMFORT ZONE 2
BUD QUOTIENT $2.25

Karaoke is on the way out in many bars. Those who know say the era of the customer-entertainer is coming to a close. I guess no one has revealed this to the clientele at Sneakers Sports Saloon. As it is with most Maryland watering holes, Friday is the biggest night of the week, and Fridays at Sneakers is "Karaoke Nite." From 9 p.m. until closing, it's a non-stop barrage of amateurs belting out their favorites. And that should tell you what kind of bar Sneakers is; an unpretentious place with friendly, outgoing patrons.

What makes it a sports saloon? Well, the decor for one. Lining one wall are posters and current sports schedules. Across from that is the saloon's "Wall of Fame," displaying such mementos as one of Jim Palmer's 1968 jerseys, an autographed Yaz poster, and a Brooks Robinson photo that was signed and dated by the Oriole third baseman on the day of his induction to the Hall of Fame.

Unlike other sports bar that combine sports graphic with beer advertising, Sneakers is all sports except for one little neon Bud sign, but that doesn't mean that Budweiser dominates the bill of fare there. Imported brews beat out the domestics 17 to 11 (and that's including two homegrown N\As), plus Bass and dark Dortmunder flow from the tap. The full gamut of California's Blossom Hill wines are served by the drink, and frozen drinks abound in the summer, topped by a Frozen Señorita Margarita made with Cuervo 1800 for $4.75 (you gotta pay for the good stuff).

Six monitors and a projection TV are connected to three different cable boxes for non-stop sports, and a large area which once served as a Pappy's Pizza kitchen is now used as a well-lit darts arena, Howard County's largest.

During the winter months, the bar is kept warm by a mammoth free-standing fireplace, and all customers are invited to a free bull roast on every sport's bar's finest day - Super Bowl Sunday.

Although a full listing of light fare is offered, the chief choice is wings. Over 75 pounds of the fiery appetizers are sold on each weekend night. Burgers topped with blue & bacon are also a best bet.

BEST TIME TO VISIT

The place fills quickly on Friday (Karaoke Nite). Better get there by six.

HOURS: Mon.-Sat. 11:30-2; Sun 4-2 except football season (1-2)

HAPPY HOUR: Mon.-Fri. discount drinks

ENTERTAINMENT: Sat. live top-40; Fri. karaoke.

ACCEPTABLE PLASTIC: V,MC,AE

KENT COUNTY

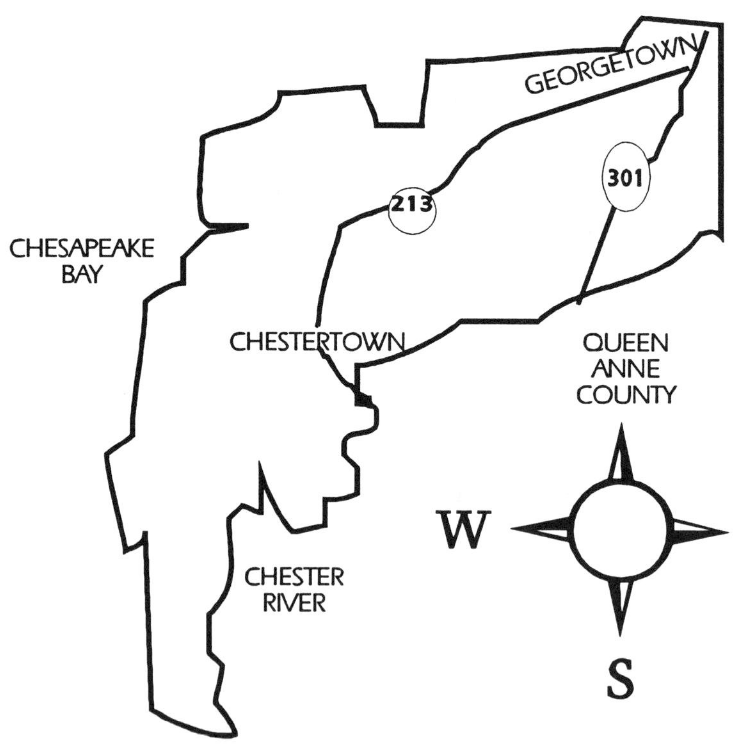

AREA: 284 Sq. Miles
Population: 17,300

ANDY'S

337 1/2 High Street
Chestertown, MD
(410) 778-6779

YUPPIE APPEAL 5
MUNCH FACTOR 5
COMFORT ZONE 5
BUD QUOTIENT $2.00

Fives across the board! A perfect score. Does that mean it doesn't get any better than Andy's?

No. It just means that the place aced the three subjective categories that I chose to highlight. Besides, a perfect bar would have a *Bud Quotient* of $0.05. But let me explain those Fives.

YUPPIE APPEAL - **5**: Uproot this bar and put it, exactly as it is, in Georgetown (D.C.), Canton, Fells Point or any other yuppie enclave, and the place would gain immediate acceptance. The bulk of its patrons now are yuppies-in-training, students of Washington College, Maryland oldest and, arguably, most expensive learning institution.

MUNCH FACTOR - **5**: Wanna talk pub food? How about mushroom & liver pate', spinach and dilled havarti sandwiches, or spinach and ricotta quiche? Too outre for you? Then how about a fresh-dough pizza or a burger? It's all gourmet pub food instead of modified restaurant offerings.

COMFORT ZONE - **5**: In the back room at Andy's, where the patrons retreat once the music starts, there's this big old fireplace and $10,000 (give or take a thou) worth of Victorian couches and loveseats, Queen Anne chairs, overstuffed recliners, and end tables with lamps. It doesn't get any more comfortable than this.

Over the years, Andy's has established itself as a major Eastern Shore music venue featuring an eclectic mix of artists such as the sister act, *disappear fear.*

Music plays Thursday through Saturdays. On Thursdays, it's jazz or solo acoustic, and the music's free. Fridays, it's easy listening acoustic, with louder and livelier dance tunes on Saturday. Plan to shell out a couple bucks for cover on Friday and Saturday night.

Unfortunately, I'm running out of room, so I can't go into detail about the two huge Ginza Boule machines inside Andy's. It's high-tech shuffleboard for the 90's, and found no where else in the state (at present: spring 1992), but it's sure to catch on.

Check it out.

BEST TIME TO VISIT

Get there around 6 on a Friday evening for Happy Hour munchies. Play a game or two of Ginza Boule, then grab a good sofa before the music starts.

HOURS: Mon.-Fri. 4-2; Sat. 4-1; closed Sun.

HAPPY HOUR: Mon.-Fri. 4-7 50 cents off all drinks

ENTERTAINMENT: Thurs.-Sat. live rock, progressive or modern

ACCEPTABLE PLASTIC: V,MC

KITTY KNIGHT HOUSE

Route 213
Georgetown, MD
(410) 648-5777 (410) 275-2000

YUPPIE APPEAL 4
MUNCH FACTOR 2
COMFORT ZONE 4
BUD QUOTIENT $2.50

Do you know who Kitty Knight is? No, she's not Ted Knight's wife. She's this woman who stood up the British Navy (or so the story goes). They say that in 1813, British Troops (under the command of Admiral Cockburn) were travelling up the Sassafras River and burning down everything along the way. But when they came to Kitty Knight's house, she refused to leave her home, and the British admiral refused to burn down Kitty's house with her still in it (history recalls her as quite a looker).

Today, Kitty's house is the oldest survivor in Georgetown and the place contains an inn, a restaurant and a tavern you shouldn't miss.

During the summer, all drinking activity centers around the Kitty Knight House's outdoor deck and its gazebo overlooking the Sassafras River and Georgetown Marina. Blender drinks and fresh-squeezed OJ creations are the top picks there and the view from the deck is fine. But there are bigger decktop bars with bigger views nearby.

When the temperature drops, the bar scene at the Kitty Knight House shifts inside - and this is definitely the time to pay the place a visit.

Their Admiral Cockburn's Tavern (named after the man who decided not to torch the place) is a wonderful sanctuary in the wintertime. With its low ceiling criss-crossed with massive black beams and thick, wooden bar and backbar, it's exactly like one of those look-but-don't-touch taverns in Colonial Williamsburg. About the only thing in the place that's not made of wood or glass is the hammered copper bar surface.

Dimly lit, with the huge fireplace as the major source of illumination, the Admiral Cockburn would be the ideal spot for a thick, black brew on a bitter winter's night. But Heineken and Molson is as exotic as the brew gets there, and only domestic brews pour from the three taps.

The sandwiches available at the tavern, however, are on the hearty side; stuffed with backfin crabcake, six-ounces of freshly ground beef or Cajun-spiced chicken.

HOURS: Mon.-Thurs. 4-12; Fri-Sat. 4-1
Oct. 20-May 1 indoors

HAPPY HOUR: Mon.-Fri. 5-7 discount drinks and free hot munchies

ENTERTAINMENT: Fri.-Sat. (summer); Sat. (winter) top-40 DJ

ACCEPTABLE PLASTIC: V,MC,AE

BEST TIME TO VISIT

If I haven't already convinced you to go there when the weather is at its coldest, I don't know any way else to put it.

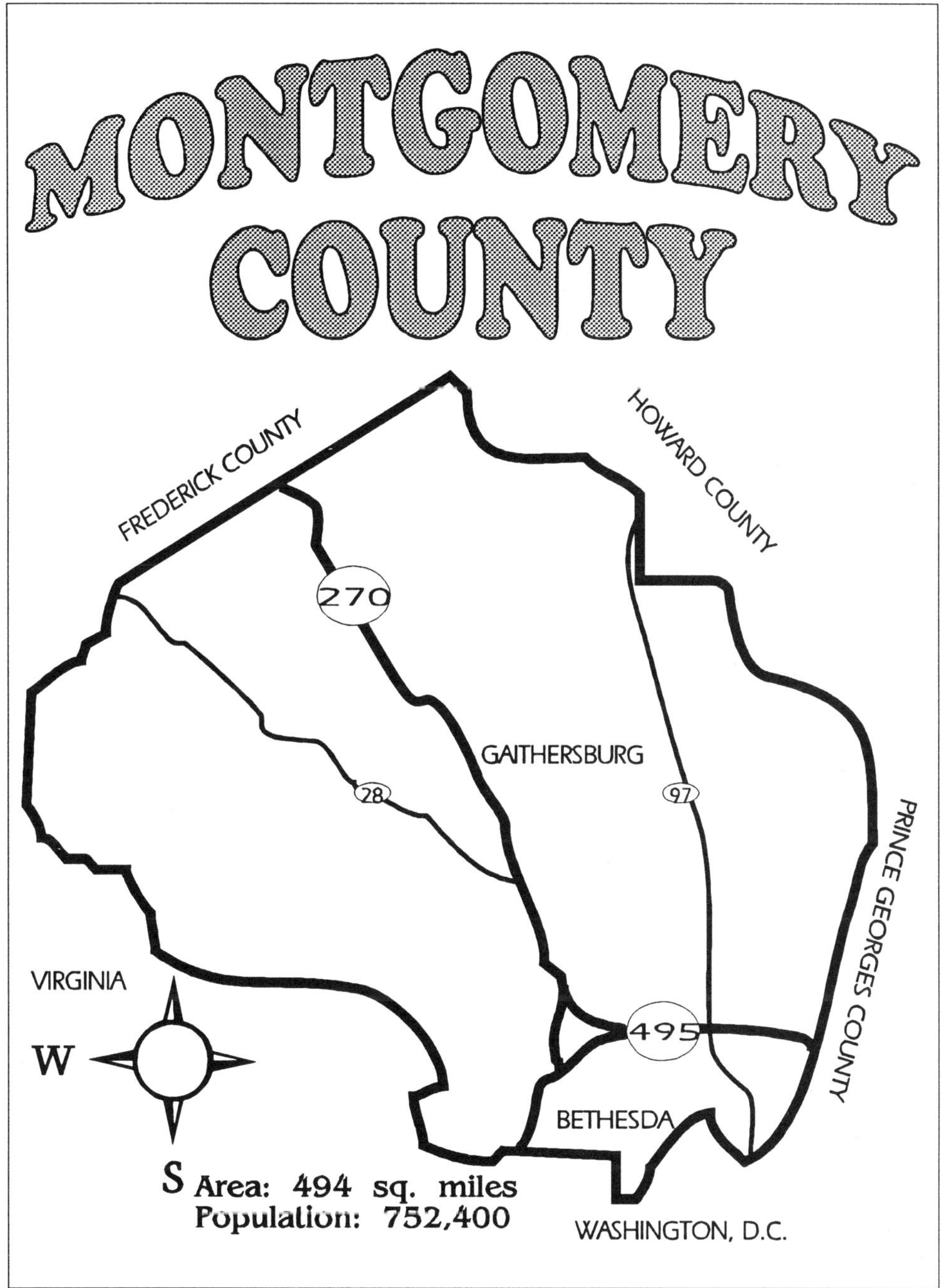
MONTGOMERY
COUNTY
FREDERICK COUNTY
HOWARD COUNTY
270
GAITHERSBURG
28
97
PRINCE GEORGES COUNTY
VIRGINIA
W
495
BETHESDA
S
Area: 494 sq. miles
Population: 752,400
WASHINGTON, D.C.

MALARKEY'S SALOON

7201 Wisconsin Avenue
Bethesda, MD
(301) 951-9000

YUPPIE APPEAL 5
MUNCH FACTOR 3
COMFORT ZONE 3
BUD QUOTIENT $2.81

Bethesda/Chevy Chase: Maryland's primo yuppie/big-money enclave filled with more white collars than The Vatican. All of the bars along and adjacent to Wisconsin Avenue get an automatic "5" on the Yuppie Appeal simply because an establishment unable to attract the area businessmen and residents could never survive there.

Malarkey's Cafe & Saloon has survived for more than five years, and for the last two years, the place has been proclaimed the "One of the Best Places to Meet Women in Metro D.C." by the *Washingtonian Magazine*, according to the manager.

Malarkey's is a big, clean and airy establishment where the crowd at the bar can freely mingle with the patrons at the surrounding tables. It's a beer crowd that inhabits the saloon and, to accommodate them, there are eight different drafts including Bass, Guinness, Moosehead and Old Heurich. And for designated drivers or those who prefer a non-alcoholic brew, Malarkey's offers a choice of four including draft O'Doul's.

Five wines are served by the glass there, and since the Bethesdan is a breed of bargoer who prefers to order his liquor by name (e.g. "Gimme an Absolut & grapefruit), the backbar has a vast selection of the high-dollar beverages.

Malarkey's pub menu, like its bar menu, reflects the taste of the young pros who fill the place. Sandwiches feature fillings that have been grilled, blackened and Cajunized. The salad list feature Caesars topped with such goodies as grilled chicken and shrimp. And Malarkey's boasts the hottest (spicy hot) potato skins in town.

Although Bethesda food & drink prices are anything but cheap (check out the *Bud Quotient*), the cost can be reasonable if you know when to go. Tuesday night is "Recession Nite," which means all beers and burgers sell for half price (e.g. a 6-oz. bacon cheeseburger for under $3). And on Friday, the food from a 12-foot hot/cold buffet is free.

When the weather warms, Malarkey's 95-seat sidewalk cafe is a great place to sit back and watch the Teutonic statusmobiles and limos go by.

HOURS: Mon.-Thurs. 11:30-1:30; Fri. 11-2:30; Sat. 6-2:30; closed Sun.

HAPPY HOUR: Mon.-Fri. 5-7 discount beer

ENTERTAINMENT: Thurs. DJ; Fri. live progressive; Sat. live classic rock

ACCEPTABLE PLASTIC: All but AE

BEST TIME TO VISIT

Thursday's Ladies Night is usually a standing-room-only affair. Get there before nine or wait in line.

NANTUCKET LANDING

4723 Elm Street
Bethesda, MD
(301) 654-7979

YUPPIE APPEAL 5
MUNCH FACTOR 3
COMFORT ZONE 3
BUD QUOTIENT $2.75

The barrooms inside Nantucket Landing has been around a while, though not under that name. It originated as the Orchid VII, and later became Flaps Up. The owner of the bar's newest incarnation has kept all of the good stuff like the English antique oak backbar on the first floor and the mammoth ornate stained glass skylight (reputed to have been salvaged from a Manhattan mansion) above the second-floor bar, and he cleaned up, refurbished or threw out everything else, turning the place into a classy and classic watering hole.

During the summer, the bar is the scene for frozen specialty drinks - over 25 varieties. Although the beer selection is rather small (two domestic drafts and about a dozen bottles), most of the weekly promos revolve around those malt beverages - Bethesda is a beer-drinkin' town. On Monday, Nantucket Landing patrons play "Beat the Clock," by going after 50-cent drafts from 5-7, $1 drafts from 7-9, and $1.50 16-ounce drafts from 9 until closing. Dollar drafts on Wednesdays attract huge crowds that fill both the downstairs and upstairs lounges from 4 until 2. And on Thursdays, Old Heurich (a tasty and creamy local microbrew) sells for the same price as Bud, plus the bar features a new strange brew (strange to Bethesdans) like Texas' Lone Star and Australia's Redback wheat at a discount.

Beach parties are staged every Saturday at Nantucket Landing, and guest bartenders man the taps every Tuesday night.

Chicken tenders (not the frozen jobs), deep-fried in a beer batter and served with a warm Dijon-honey mustard, is the Nantucket's top finger food. Grilled chicken topped Caesar salads are presented in a tortilla shell bowl. Burgers, served in a toasted onion roll, are half-pounders, and the grilled sandwiches are served between slabs of fresh French bread.

Serving as overflow space for weekend and Dollar Draft Night crowds, and as a dining room during the afternoons, Nantucket's second floor has become a popular banquet facilities for groups who want a non-hotel atmosphere.

BEST TIME TO VISIT

The place goes crazy on Wednesday night when draft flows for a buck.

HOURS: Mon.-Thurs. 11:30-1; Fri. 11:30-2; Sat. 5-2; Sun. private parties

HAPPY HOUR: Mon.-Fri. 4-7 all drinks half-price

ENTERTAINMENT: Wed.-Sat. DJ rock & dancing

ACCEPTABLE PLASTIC: V,MC,AE

ROY'S PLACE

2 E. Diamond Avenue
Gaithersburg, MD
(301) 948-5548

YUPPIE APPEAL	3
MUNCH FACTOR	5
COMFORT ZONE	3
BUD QUOTIENT	No Bud

For those evenings when all you want is an icy draft in one hand and a great sandwich in the other, I know the perfect spot.

If you're not from Gaithersburg, you'll never find the place, so call for directions - and go there because what the Corner Bar (featured herein) is to spirits, the Last Chance (featured herein) is to draft, and La Trattoria (featured herein) is to wine, Roy's Place is to sandwiches.

The tavern has an "old west" kind of feel. The large dining area is filled with small checkered tablecloth covered tables and old wooden chairs. Almost every square inch of the wall space is covered with framed Americana (defunct magazine covers, turn-of-the-century newspaper headlines, and old advertisements) plus 50 or so magazine and newspaper reviews (plus the one I wrote in 1981 for the *Frederick News-Post*). Tiffany swag lamps and old-time ceiling fans hang from the ceiling.

A dark hardwood partition separates the main dining hall from the bar/tavern area which is filled with more framed stuff along with rows of old and dusty liquor bottles.

There's a full selection of liquor at the bar from which the bartenders construct all of the usual drinks, plus the most expensive mixed drink in the house: a "Roy's Knockup" made with vodka, Amaretto, brandy, cherry kijafa, OJ, sour mix and grenadine and served in a 16-ounce beer glass. Wine there is the usual stuff. The drink to drink at Roy's Place is beer - draft beer (Bass, Watney's and three different Michs) served in a frosted 16-oz. mug. And the food to eat at Roy's Place is a sandwich, commonplace fare which has elevated to an art form.

Roy's Place's menu lists more than 170 different meals encased between slices of rye, wheat, pumpernickel, white and French breads ranging in price from $4.65 to $16.30. Among the more exotic entries are the "Fred Ward," a four-decker filled with lobster and crab salads, ham, chicken and veggies boasting the highest price, the "Bender Schmender," an 18-inch high five-decker club stuffed with corned beer, turkey, roast pork, pate, brisket, and on and on.

HOURS: Mon.-Thurs. 11-11; Fri. - Sat. 11-12; Sun. 12-11

HAPPY HOUR: Mon.-Sun. 2:15-6 discount drinks

ENTERTAINMENT: Jukebox

ACCEPTABLE PLASTIC: All but CB

BEST TIME TO VISIT

To avoid the crowds, visit Roy's Place during the week before 7.

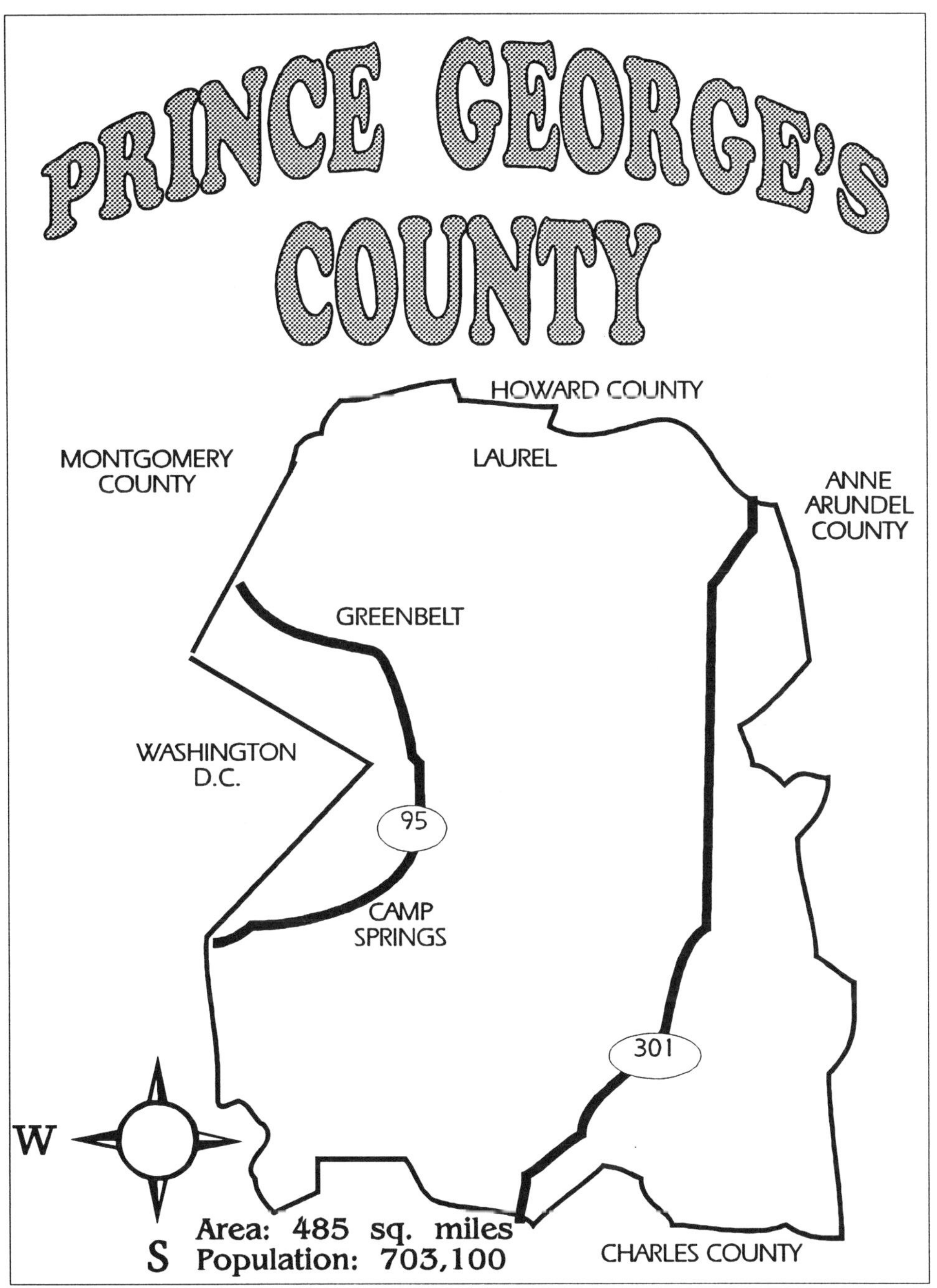
PRINCE GEORGE'S COUNTY
HOWARD COUNTY
MONTGOMERY COUNTY
LAUREL
ANNE ARUNDEL COUNTY
GREENBELT
WASHINGTON D.C.
95
CAMP SPRINGS
301
W
S
Area: 485 sq. miles
Population: 703,100
CHARLES COUNTY

BOWIE INN

6868 Racetrack Road
Bowie, MD
(301) 262-5666

YUPPIE APPEAL 2
MUNCH FACTOR 3
COMFORT ZONE 2
BUD QUOTIENT $1.90

The 1970s and early 1980s was the era of the small Bowie bar. Every afternoon for a third of the Maryland horse racing season (Bowie shared the year's card with Pimlico and Laurel), the small P.G. County town would be filled with bettors in mismatched suits. When the day's racing was over, they needed places to drown their sorrows and forget how much they lost. And when racing disappeared from Bowie, so too went many of the small watering holes that made their living on the betting men.

Of all the bars that catered to Bowie race track fans, the Bowie Inn was the most popular, and it lost the most when the nearby track folded. But instead of giving in, like its contemporaries, the Bowie Inn strengthened its kitchen and thrived.

The Bowie Inn today is the type of establishment to visit when you don't feel like having lasers bounce off your leisure suit or you don't feel like subjecting yourself to 12 Karaoke renditions of *Cocaine*. You go to the Bowie Inn to eat, drink and talk - inexpensively.

The executive chef there will tell you, "Our cooking is 25 years behind the times. All our food is prepared like it was at a time before mixes." Mashed potatoes there are actual potatoes mashed on the premises. Shrimp there is not just spiced and tossed in a steamer, it's cooked in a mixture of vinegar, beer and vegetables.

At the bar, the big drinks are still the martini and Manhattan (old people's drinks), but the second generation of those old people are starting to come in, and the beverage and food menus are slowly changing. Six wines from California's Fetzer and Glen Ellen wineries have found their way into the bar, and a daily special is more likely to be broiled salmon in a white wine and mushroom sauce than meatloaf and green beans.

Old or young, the patrons at the Bowie Inn come in for the same reason - to relax and talk. The major subjects of conversation there are politics and sports - especially the ponies.

Horse racing may be gone from Bowie, but it's not forgotten.

HOURS: Mon.-Sun. 9 a.m.-12

HAPPY HOUR: Mon.-Fri. 4-7 discount drinks

ENTERTAINMENT: Jukebox

ACCEPTABLE PLASTIC: V,MC,AE

BEST TIME TO VISIT

Stop in on a Wednesday or Thursday (the inn's busiest nights) for a prime rib sandwich and a Bud.

THE HANGAR CLUB

6410 Old Branch Avenue
Camp Springs, MD
(301) 449-6970

YUPPIE APPEAL 5
MUNCH FACTOR 2
COMFORT ZONE 3
BUD QUOTIENT $2.89

Why do hundreds of women crowd into The Hangar Club three nights a week? Could it be that they flock there for the nice beer selection (over 30 brands), or perhaps they come for the food (a vast variety of finger foods and sandwiches). Or just maybe they arrive in droves to see a large variety of mesomorphic male-model types artistically drop trou.

Before there were Chippendale dancers or any other professional troupe of male strippers, there was "Body Motion - The Men of the Hangar Club." Since 1974, males have been taking it off at The Hangar before SRO crowds of screaming female patrons, from local ladies to the wives of Supreme Court Justices, and ranging in age from 18 (they can be in there, but they can't drink) to 92.

Unlike their female counterparts who mostly just bump, grind and squat (a lot of squatting and toe touching), the Hangar's male dancers perform a complete three-hour Las Vegas-type choreographed show every Thursday, Friday and Saturday night, right after the owner/emcee welcomes the audience and lays down the few simple ground rules.

On Mondays through Saturdays from lunchtime through 6:30, topless ladies take the Hangar's stage and perform in the shadow of a huge sign that reads "*Tipping performers allowed. Tips can be handed to performers or placed on the stage railing.*" Unlike the ecdysiasts of The Block who make the big bucks off stage by serving drinks and "mingling" with the customers, Hangar girls are restricted to dancing for a living.

But the Camp Spring nightclub's real raison d'etre is its male performers. The place hosts over 1,500 bachelorette parties alone each year, and all of the parties' guests of honor receive special treatment (e.g. presentation of anatomically-correct cakes) from the Hangar boys.

The deceptively large nightclub can easily accommodate over 270 patrons at its bar stools, tri-level dining area chairs and tiered theater seats, all giving an unobstructed view of the stage and the players.

BEST TIME TO VISIT

Ladies' nights are Thursdays through Saturdays. Reservation most nights are a necessity, and the best seats are snagged by 7:30.

HOURS: Mon.-Thurs. 11-2; Fri.-Sat. 11-3; Sun. 10-12:30

HAPPY HOUR: None

ENTERTAINMENT: Female and male performers

ACCEPTABLE PLASTIC: None

HAWTHORNE'S

8811 Greenbelt Road
Greenbelt, MD
(301) 552-3030

YUPPIE APPEAL 4
MUNCH FACTOR 4
COMFORT ZONE 3
BUD QUOTIENT $2.50

Every state needs a sports/art bar, and in Maryland, it's Hawthorne's. A sports/art bar? What's that?

For two years, the building that currently houses Hawthorne's was home to Curly's Garage, a theme-park of a bar carrying the automobile craze to the limit. It never really caught on. So, when Hawthorne's was conceived, there would be no overkill in the thematic sense. Instead the place would be a warm, receptive sanctuary with bare brick walls bearing century-old art works featuring the famous madams and professional ladies of turn-of-the-century Chicago, and where there weren't paintings, there would be mirrors etched with the bar's logo and framed posters of modern masterworks. That's how Hawthorne's started.

But Greenbelt is Redskin's Territory, and a few alterations were made in the interior of Hawthorne's tavern. A 10-foot projection TV (Greenbelt's only mammoth pub projection set) was added and one wall, devoted to the sports devotees, started displaying football and baseball memorabilia.

The sit-down bar inside Hawthorne's is Greenbelt's best; a huge hardwood structure with just a touch of neon overhead, and a set of illuminated central shelves which turn the different colored beverages into a light show.

Fifteen bottle brews (mostly imports) including Canada's Calgary are offered along with five drafts. There's only a Sutter Home selection for wine drinkers at the bar, but some imaginative spirit creations are offered. A Chicago Rose is a blend of Amaretto, Baileys, strawberries and cream; the Hawthorne's Hurricane is a potent melange of fruit juices, Amaretto, rum, gin and Myers's dark rum.

For those with a little extra disposable cash and a taste for something different, the kitchen has created the Chesapeake Burger: eight ounces of charbroiled beef topped with cheddar and backfin then dusted with Old Bay ($7.25). Hawthorne's tavern menu (probably the most extensive in P.G. County) starts with a dozen un-traditional bar offerings like toasted ravioli, a trio of mini Italian beef sandwiches, and it just goes on and on...

HOURS: Mon.-Sun. 11-2

HAPPY HOUR: Mon.-Fri. 4-7 discount drinks and free hot & cold munchies

ENTERTAINMENT: Thurs.-Fri. DJ rock

ACCEPTABLE PLASTIC: All but D

BEST TIME TO VISIT

Arrive an hour before any Redskin game and claim a good seat.

KANGAROO KATIE'S

7511 Greenbelt Road
Greenbelt, MD
(301) 474-9011

YUPPIE APPEAL	4
MUNCH FACTOR	4
COMFORT ZONE	3
BUD QUOTIENT	$2.85

There's just not enough room on this page to tell you about everything that goes on inside Kangaroo Katie's. You're just going to have to experience this place for yourself.

Do you like beer? There are over 120 brews from 22 different countries, plus five microbrews, seven drafts and every Aussie beer available in Maryland.

Do you like wine? There's always at least 15 different varietals, most from premium Australian (of course) vineyards.

Do you like shooters? Go there on Sunday and create your own, or select one of the standards including the house creation, *Tight Snatch.*

Do you like to try new foods? How about some alligator tail: marinated, tenderized and beer-battered strips of alligator meat deep-fried and served with cocktail sauce? Or how about some kangaroo sausage stew?

Do you like to show people how smart you are? Every Thursday at Kangaroo Katie's is team trivia night with the smartest group getting a $100 gift certificate.

Do you like bingo? No kidding! They do it on Wednesdays. It may sound lame, but it's not.

Do you like taxidermy? The place is filled with motionless marsupials (mostly roos and wallabies) plus this huge hairy Asian camel.

Do you like a choice of bars? Kangaroo Katie's offers two separate bars, mirror images of one another, each fortified with all that beer, all that wine, all those shooter fixin's and a complete spirit selection.

Do you like a little light with your music? Katie's just installed a state-of-the-art laser light system to accompany their nightly DJ offerings.

Do you like flora? Above each of the bars at Kangaroo Katie's is a jungle of potted plants surrounding a system of vertical rattan-blade fans.

There's a whole lot more going on inside this Greenbelt yuppie food & drink emporium. There isn't another club in Maryland that exerts more effort to give the customer what he wants.

BEST TIME TO VISIT

That really depends on what you like to do best. Might I suggest a rousing game of bingo on Wednesday?

HOURS: Sun.-Thurs. 11:30-1:30; Fri.-Sat. 11:30-2:30

HAPPY HOUR: Mon.-Fri. 4-7 half-price rail drinks and drafts

ENTERTAINMENT: Mon.-Sun. DJ from 9 until closing

ACCEPTABLE PLASTIC: V,MC,AE,DC

OLIVER'S SALOON

531 Main Street
Laurel, MD
(301) 490-9200

As early as a dozen years ago, Laurel was anything but a nightlife destination. Oh, there were bars, dozens of them lining Rte. 1 and out Rte. 197. They were the little dingy dives where old drunks go to die, and young rednecks go to fight. The creators of Oliver's must have known change was in the air, because in 1982 they introduced a bar that was much too nice for Laurel.

Today, all of those Route 1 hillbilly joints are gone. Laurel has changed radically during the past decade, but one thing hasn't changed. Oliver's is still the nicest pub in town.

Wines from producers such as Robert Mondavi and Napa Ridge are served up by the glass there. When you order a screwdriver or a vodka & grapefruit, the bartenders squeezes fresh fruit for the juice. And you have a choice of 10 different draft brews including Sam Adams, Rolling Rock and the house brew, Oliver's Ale.

HOURS: Sun.-Thurs. 11-2; Fri.-Sat. 11-3

HAPPY HOUR: Mon.-Fri. 3-7 80-cent drafts, munchies

ENTERTAINMENT: Fri. DJ rock; Sat. live contemporary, rock

ACCEPTABLE PLASTIC: V,MC,AE

YUPPIE APPEAL 3
MUNCH FACTOR 3
COMFORT ZONE 3
BUD QUOTIENT $2.25

Nacho Grandes there are the 10-ingredient variety. Burgers are a half pound of freshly ground top sirloin. And all of the overstuffed sandwiches (nearly 20 different creations) are made with home-baked breads. On Wednesdays, Oliver's veers away from the traditional pub food route by offering a complete steak Diane dinner (cooked tableside) for only $12.95, or a pot of Maryland-style bouillabaisse (lobster, shrimp, mussels, crab and oysters in a biting broth).

With most of the action taking place at the large centrally-located bar, Oliver's is the closest you can get to a *Cheers* environment in Laurel. The place has its "Norms" and "Cliffs," but a large portion of the clientele are the white collar types from nearby business parks and government offices.

To lure in customers on Monday (the slowest day of the week), Oliver's treats them to free steamed crabs during the summer, and free steamed and raw shellfish in the "R" months. And Thursdays are always "Beach Nights," starring four or five fresh-fruit daiquiris.

By the end of 1992, Oliver's will have finished it's renovation which will double their capacity. They need the room.

BEST TIME TO VISIT

It all comes together at Oliver's on Friday evenings.

O'TOOLE'S PUB

9634 Fort Meade Road
Laurel, MD
(301) 498-7427

YUPPIE APPEAL 4
MUNCH FACTOR 4
COMFORT ZONE 3
BUD QUOTIENT $2.85

Yeah, I know O'Toole's is a chain, and I said at the front of the book that I wasn't doing chains. So, I lied. O'Toole's has something that other bars don't, and I feel it's worth mentioning.

Some Maryland bars have "Trivia Nite" where small groups compete for cash prizes or gift certificates by answering original questions concocted by the establishment, and that's ok. Some clubs have the audacity to break out the *Trivial Pursuit* cards for their competition, and that stinks. At O'Toole's, you compete against trivia buffs from all over America and Canada via satellite at a game called Countdown, and that's fun.

Every hour or so at O'Toole's, a new Countdown game is played. Patrons play the game utilizing a small keyboard with a stubby antenna that's linked into the system. The questions (15 per game) are *Final Jeopardy*-hard and multiple-choice, and scoring is based on not just knowing the right answer, but answering quickly as well.

Every Tuesday evening, there's a national championship Countdown game with the high scorers winning microwaves or Sony Watchmans. Recently, a 19-inch color TV was won by an O'Toole's player.

There's more to O'Toole's than the Countdown game (although that is it's singlemost neatest facet). At the 90-foot serpentine (wavy) bar or at the tables surrounding the huge four-sided woodburning fireplace, customers have their choice of over 30 beers - eight keg brews - to accompany a great selection of appetizers including their "10-Layer Dip," nacho grande ingredients all layered together in a bowl with a basket of fresh tortilla chips on the side. Ribs, a large selection of sandwiches, Mexican cuisine and "Hearty Classics," like mac & cheese are also on the menu.

On Tuesday, Thursday (Ladies' Night: half-price drinks), and Saturday, a DJ spins top-40 dance tunes, and the music is live on Friday. And if you're on a limited budget, wings are just 15 cents apiece on Tuesday.

BEST TIME TO VISIT

Try to make it there by five on Tuesday for a few practice games of Countdown before the championship starts (watch out for a team of five U. of M. professors called "The Quarks").

HOURS: Mon.-Sun. 11-2

HAPPY HOUR: Mon.-Sun. 4-8 discount drinks (buffet Mon.-Fri.)

ENTERTAINMENT: Sat. karaoke; Tues. DJ rock

ACCEPTABLE PLASTIC: All

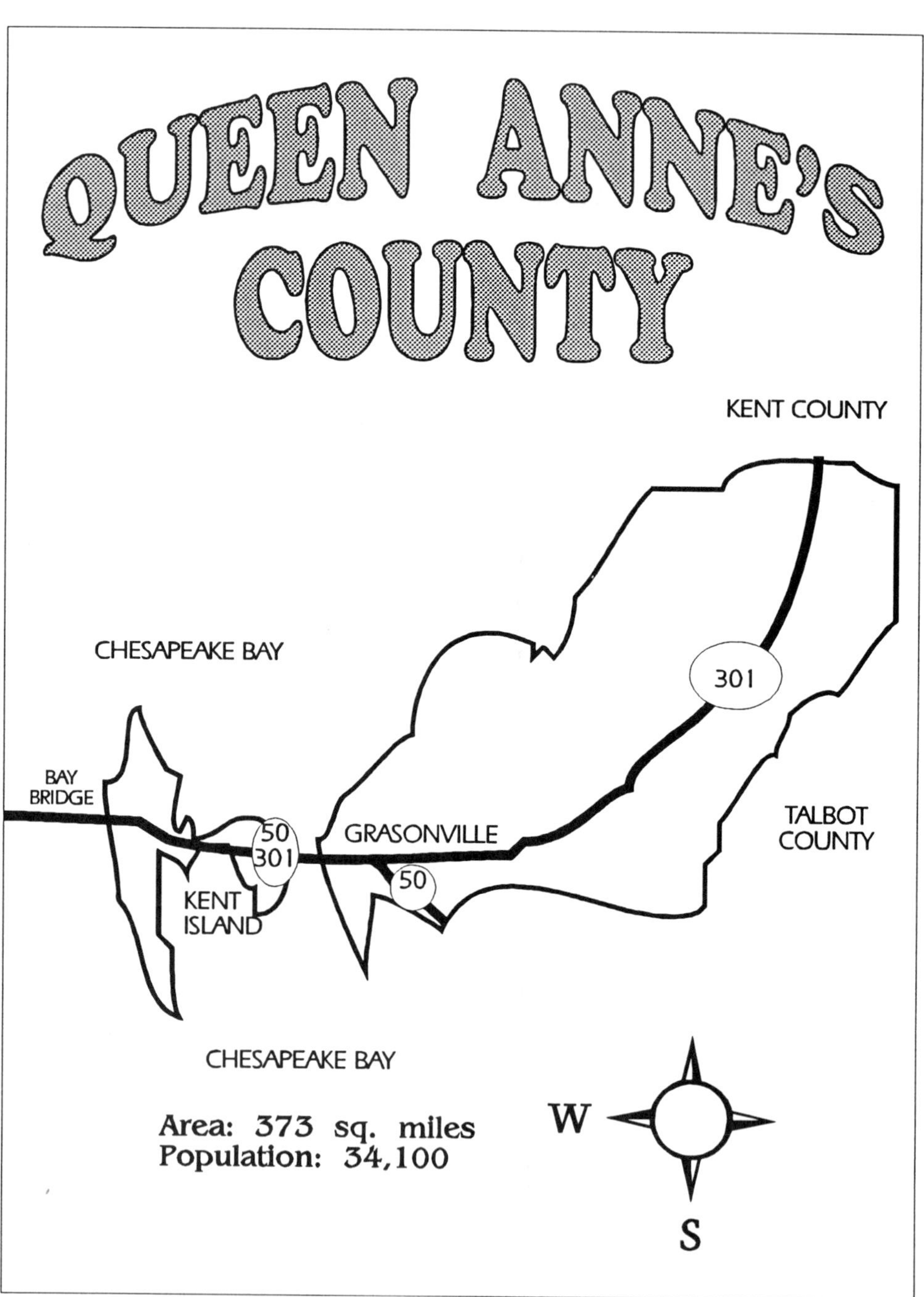
QUEEN ANNE'S COUNTY
KENT COUNTY
CHESAPEAKE BAY
301
BAY BRIDGE
50
301
GRASONVILLE
TALBOT COUNTY
50
KENT ISLAND
CHESAPEAKE BAY
Area: 373 sq. miles
Population: 34,100
W
S

RED EYE'S DOCK BAR

Route 50 at Kent Narrows
Grasonville, MD
(410) 827-3937

YUPPIE APPEAL 4
MUNCH FACTOR 4
COMFORT ZONE 3
BUD QUOTIENT $2.85

For lack of a better phrase, I'll call it the "Tiki Bar Conundrum," (TBC) named after the Tiki Bar on Solomons Island. On that small Calvert County resort enclave, there are about a dozen food and drink operations, many with excellent menus and beautiful decors. But where do the majority of Solomons Island summer visitors go? The Tiki Bar, an open-air watering hole where the decor is mostly customer's knick knacks and the cuisine is popcorn (although they have an awesome Mai Tai).

On Kent Island, a perfect example of the TBC is Red Eye's Dock Bar, an 80-seat, open-to-the-elements warm-weather watering hole whose main decor enhancement are a few hundred feet of fish net and an antique breast enlarger (don't ask). But on weekend evenings, it not unusual to find crowds of over 1,000 crunched at the bar and the surrounding deck and piers. Red Eye's is not just your garden variety waterfront bar. It's an event.

What's perhaps most amazing is that Red Eye's is not a tenny-bopper hangout. Those weekend patrons range in age from 35 to 70. They come to hear the classic rock (1960's & 70's) and Motown sounds on Fridays and Saturdays. And on Sundays, they come to see the girls.

A bikini contest, with prizes ranging from $50 to $250, is staged on Red Eye's pier each Sunday. Although the competition is open to all, wannabe exhibitionists should be warned that the majority of the competitors are T&A-intensive pros who do this kind of stuff for a living. On September 20, all of the weekly winners of the bikini contest will compete in the finals. If you plan on getting a good seat for that grand finale, I suggest you get there early (like September 19).

There's a full bar at Red Eye's, but most come here for the beer (a choice of two imports and six domestics) and shooters. On Sundays, designated drivers are offered all the free sodas and O'Doul's N\A brew they can hold. Food there is mostly burgers and picnic fare. But the main attraction is neither food nor drink. People go to Red Eye's to BE at the Red Eye's.

BEST TIME TO VISIT

Sunday afternoons and evenings are what Red Eye's is all about.

HOURS: Mon.-Sun. 11-2

HAPPY HOUR: None

ENTERTAINMENT: Fri.-Sun. live rock, Motown

ACCEPTABLE PLASTIC: V,MC,AE

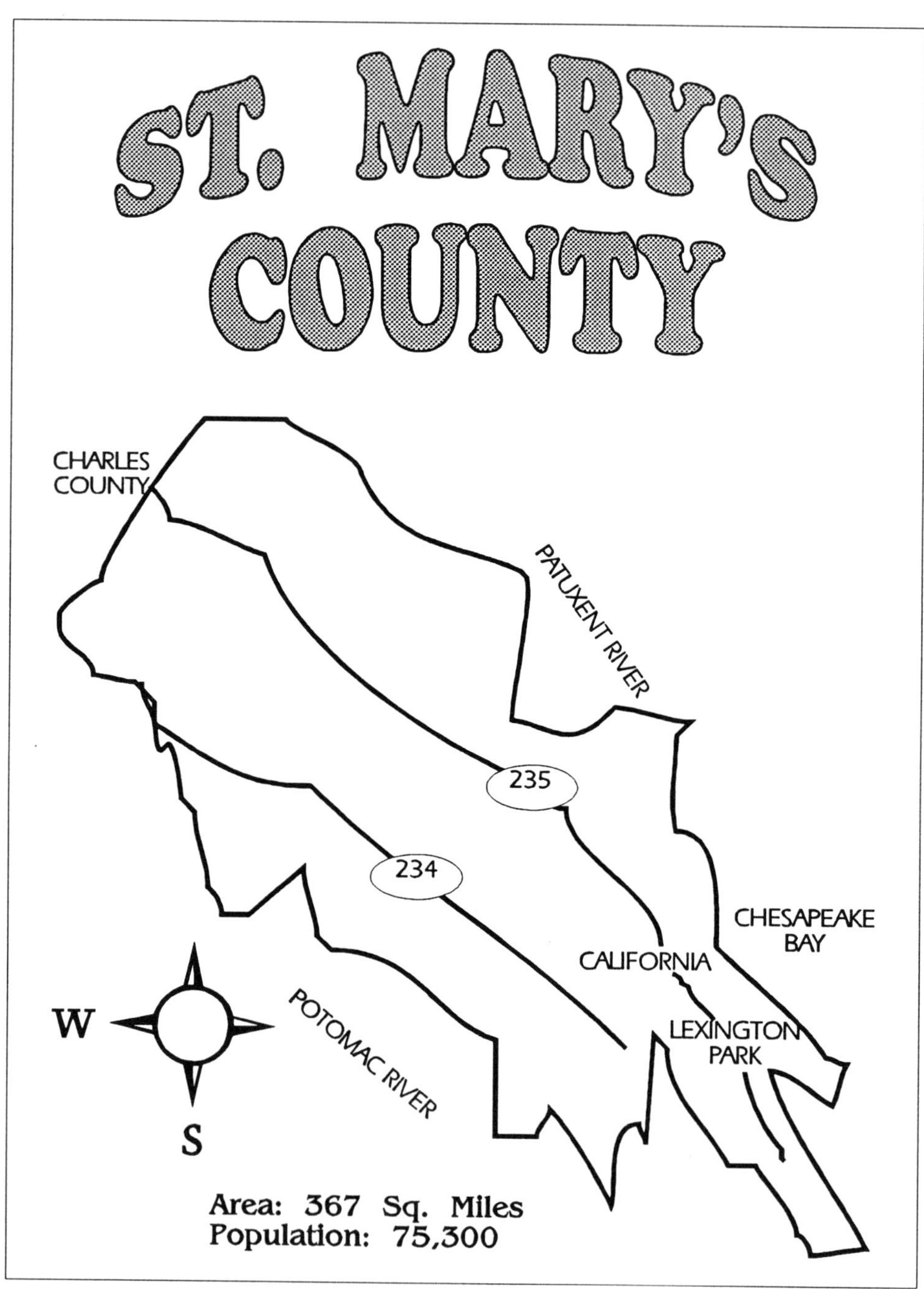
ST. MARY'S COUNTY
CHARLES COUNTY
PATUXENT RIVER
235
234
CHESAPEAKE BAY
CALIFORNIA
LEXINGTON PARK
W
S
POTOMAC RIVER
Area: 367 Sq. Miles
Population: 75,300

CADILLAC JACK'S

1603 Great Mills Road
Lexington Park, MD
(301) 862-4703

YUPPIE APPEAL 3
MUNCH FACTOR 0
COMFORT ZONE 3
BUD QUOTIENT $2.25

Jack bought this bar in Lexington Park, but he couldn't hang around. So he found someone to manage the place, and he took off to see the world. At least once a week, Cadillac Jack's manager receives a telegram from the owner. And small packages from Jack containing currency from Bali, theater bills from London or brothel vouchers from Thailand arrive at the St. Mary's County nightclub. Jack just wants everyone there to know that he's having a good time.

Of course, there is no Jack. There's only Ruth, the owner/manager of Cadillac Jack's, who plays out the "roving absentee owner" theme to the hilt. The walls are filled with souvenirs and mementos (including a lace undies collection) amassed by the travelling lothario, and phone calls at the bar are answered with "Cadillac Jack's. Jack's not here."

The 200-seat nightclub contains a DJ booth that's made up of the front and rear halves of a real pink Cadillac, with turn signals, headlights and brake lights flickering to the beat of the music. There's also a large freestanding fireplace within, plus a darts area, two pool tables, and walls filled with Cadillac parts and framed photo of 1950s and 60s film and TV stars.

Thursdays find the place packed with patrons drinking 50-cent drafts. And the only food to appear there (except for popcorn) is a Friday night nacho bar for a buck. But imported beer drinkers will find the place to their liking with 15 non-domestics on the menu.

The house drink, Pink Cadillac, a concoction of Peachtree, Crantasia (cranberry schnapps), pineapple juice & grenadine, is a popular pour there, as are Ponzai Punch (?) and the Malibu Breeze. And even though Ruth has tried her hardest to introduce her customers to the finer wines, those little bottles of Sutter Home are still the rage.

Once a month, Cadillac Jack's is the site of an elaborate theme party which could involve patrons arriving in their pajamas, or an Easter egg hunt complete with cash prizes for finding the golden egg.

BEST TIME TO VISIT

Get there before nine on Friday or Saturday for a good seat. Call to see what the next theme party will be.

HOURS: Tues.-Thurs. 6-2; Fri. 4-2; Sat. 8-2; closed Sun.-Mon.

HAPPY HOUR: Fri. 4-8 discount drinks

ENTERTAINMENT: Tues.-Sat. DJ rock

ACCEPTABLE PLASTIC: V,MC

NOKLEBY'S NIGHT CLUB

2052 Wildewood Center
California, MD
(301) 862-2330

YUPPIE APPEAL 4
MUNCH FACTOR 4
COMFORT ZONE 4
BUD QUOTIENT $2.10

While sitting at Nokleby's bar one early afternoon, I noticed a steady stream of waitress emerging from the kitchen door each bearing plates piled high with roast beef and mashed potatoes drenched in gravy along with a more than healthy serving of string beans. I looked down at the menu on the bar and read that entree's price - $3.95.

Nokleby's may be St. Mary's County's glitziest night club, but its a lot more. Located in one of Maryland's more economically depressed areas, it serves up huge portions of great food for a pittance. Overstuffed sandwiches, available all night, peak in price at $3.75 for a steak and cheese, and there are plenty of the true finger foods from which to choose including honey wings and nachos.

Located in one of Maryland's most predominantly blue-collar counties, Nokleby's has it's own pool room - perhaps not the largest, but the most lavishly assembled billiard arena in Southern Maryland. Small cafe tables with comfortably upholstered chairs surround the trio of well-maintained, well-lighted pool tables, and the walls are covered with hundreds of framed Redskin collectibles including old posters and signed photos.

Located in a section of Maryland only a stone's throw from Solomons Island, Nokleby's has to try harder that its southern St. Mary's County counterparts to attract and keep its customers.

Although the lacquered brass and cushioned bar stool is one great seat, the lounge, filled with the same comfortable chairs as those in the pool room, is the place to lounge and settle back with a Nokleby shooter or one of their infamous "Yeast Infections," a sweet concoction of Peachtree, coconut rum, pineapple juice and cream. All shooters there go for a buck fifty.

Despite its locale, Nokleby's doesn't serve up country or country rock or southern rock on the weekends. It's live rock and roll all the way. Killians (a most popular Southern Maryland draft selection) and two other domestics are found tap at the bar, along with all the spirits you know.

HOURS: Mon.-Sat. 10-2; closed Sun.

HAPPY HOUR: Mon.-Fri. 4-7 discount drinks

ENTERTAINMENT: Fri.-Sat. DJ or live rock & roll

ACCEPTABLE PLASTIC: AE

BEST TIME TO VISIT

Friday Happy Hours come replete with free subs, meatballs and the like. Catch it before the show.

WASHINGTON COUNTY

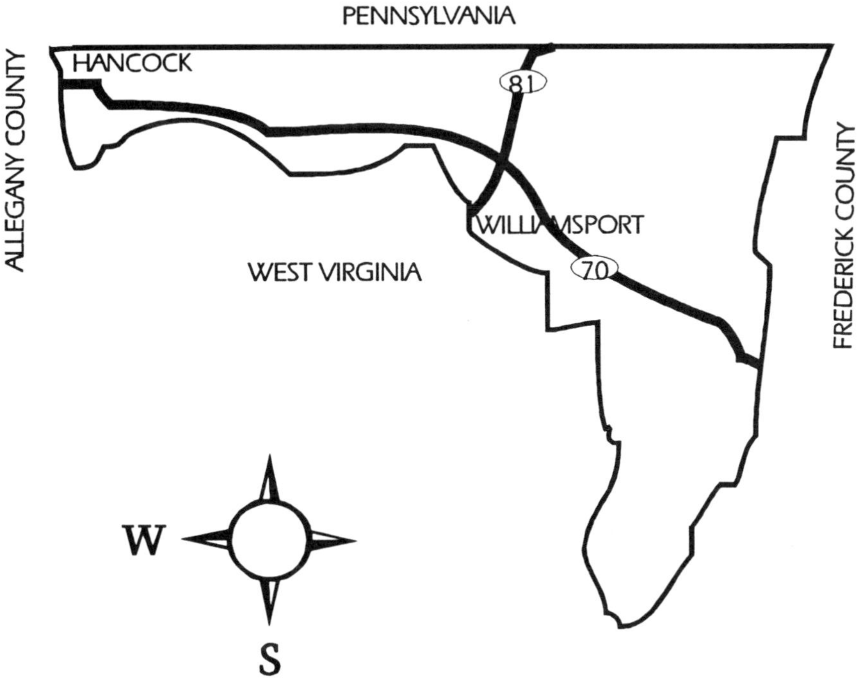

PENNSYLVANIA
ALLEGANY COUNTY
HANCOCK
81
WILLIAMSPORT
70
WEST VIRGINIA
FREDERICK COUNTY
W
S

Area: 462 sq. miles
Population: 119.800

HANCOCK TOWN TAVERN

15 W. Main Street
Hancock, MD
(301) 678-6732

YUPPIE APPEAL	1
MUNCH FACTOR	0
COMFORT ZONE	1
BUD QUOTIENT	$1.20

The next time you find yourself out west (beyond Hagerstown, that is), stop in the Hancock Town Tavern, one of the most unusual "Theme Bars" west of Rte. 81.

No, you're not going to find 101 beers from which to choose. They have 12 brews with the most exotic being Old German. There's not an import in the house.

No, you're not going to find any exotic spirits. There's no Absolut, Tanqueray, or single malt scotches on the backbar. This is a bar for Seagram 7, Gilbey's vodka and Canadian Mist.

No, you're not going to find any specialty foods on the menu. Ham or chicken salad sandwiches are there along with those two gallon jugs of pickled eggs and hot baloney. That's about it.

So, why go to the Hancock Town Tavern? The answer will come to you as soon as you walk into the place. The wall behind the bar is filled with over 200 Wild Turkey and Jim Beam decanters, each with a different wild animal theme, and on a centrally-located, glass-enclosed shelf are nearly a dozen different bourbon ceramics of Elvis (some of those decanters are worth a small fortune). But the real sights are on the other walls.

The Hancock Town Tavern is a large, clean small-town bar and its walls are filled with big game trophies - huge heads of water and cape buffalos, elands and zebras, elk and bears, plus a wildebeest, a moose with a six-foot rack and a half dozen species of rare antelope. Everywhere you look, there's another creature: an Alaskan king crab, a largemouth bass, an otter, a wild turkey, and a deer's butt. In the storage room downstairs, according to the bartender, there sits a stuffed full-length African lion and a nine-foot black bear.

This is a hunter's bar with one corner displaying framed photos of winners in the tavern's annual buck hunting contest (grand prize $150). But it's those massive African animals (hung low enough to touch) that make the Town Tavern worth a stop.

HOURS: Mon.-Sat. 8-2; Sun. 1-10

HAPPY HOUR: Tues. 4-7 discount drafts

ENTERTAINMENT: 1950's & 60's country/western jukebox

ACCEPTABLE PLASTIC: None

BEST TIME TO VISIT

If you happen to wander in there on a Friday evening and wonder what that antelope with the long spiral horns is called, the bar will be filled with regulars glad to impart their amazing zoological knowledge.

WAYSIDE INN

17116 Virginia Avenue
Williamsport, MD
(301) 582-4402

YUPPIE APPEAL 2
MUNCH FACTOR 4
COMFORT ZONE 2
BUD QUOTIENT $1.25

Money's tight in the non-resort towns of Western Maryland (the land beyond Frederick County). To keep drink prices low, nightclubs out west almost have to be subsidized by other operations. That's why all of Hagerstown's big clubs are adjuncts of national motel chains (Holiday Inn, Sheraton, Best Western, Ramada). The last attempt at a free-standing Hagerstown glitter palace was the short-lived disco, Rumors. So, how does the Wayside Inn keep its prices down and keep its head above water? Fried chicken.

In the small town of Williamsport, a few miles southwest of Hagerstown, there's the Wayside Inn, a full-tilt classic rock nightclub with drinks bearing Western Maryland price tags: domestic beers for $1.25, imported brews for $1.85, and big shooters for a buck fifty, as examples.

The Wayside Inn management can hold down the price of drinking because the place is also a largely successful local catering company specializing in fresh (never frozen) fried chicken. That chicken is also available inside a large tavern menu featuring 20 sandwiches (including a cheese-bacon-ham-topped burger for $2.65) and a dozen hot and cold sides (featuring a 90-cent broccoli & cauliflower salad dressed with bacon & cheese). And what other Maryland nightclub bar can afford to offer a half-pound of homestyle fried chicken livers (a great match with a pint of Grolsch) for $2.

Specialty drinks abound at the Wayside's long, comfortable bar with the most popular by far being an indigenous concoction called The Slide. Made up in half-gallon batches, those blue-green shooters containing 10 different spirits including Southern Comfort, Old Crow, Yukon Jack, blueberry schnapps and 151-proof Bacardi, sell for $1.50. Rocket Fuel, another $1.50 shooter, contains 11 different name brand spirits.

Local and regional rock bands like Cracked Actor, Never Never and The Road Ducks take the Wayside Inn's stage on the weekends, and it's not unusual for the place to sell out by 8 p.m. on Saturday nights when Never Never is in town.

BEST TIME TO VISIT

For an inexpensive evening of food, drink and live rock, get there before 9 on Friday.

HOURS: Mon.-Sat. 9 a.m.-2; closed Sun.

HAPPY HOUR: None

ENTERTAINMENT: Fri.-Sat. live classic rock

ACCEPTABLE PLASTIC: None

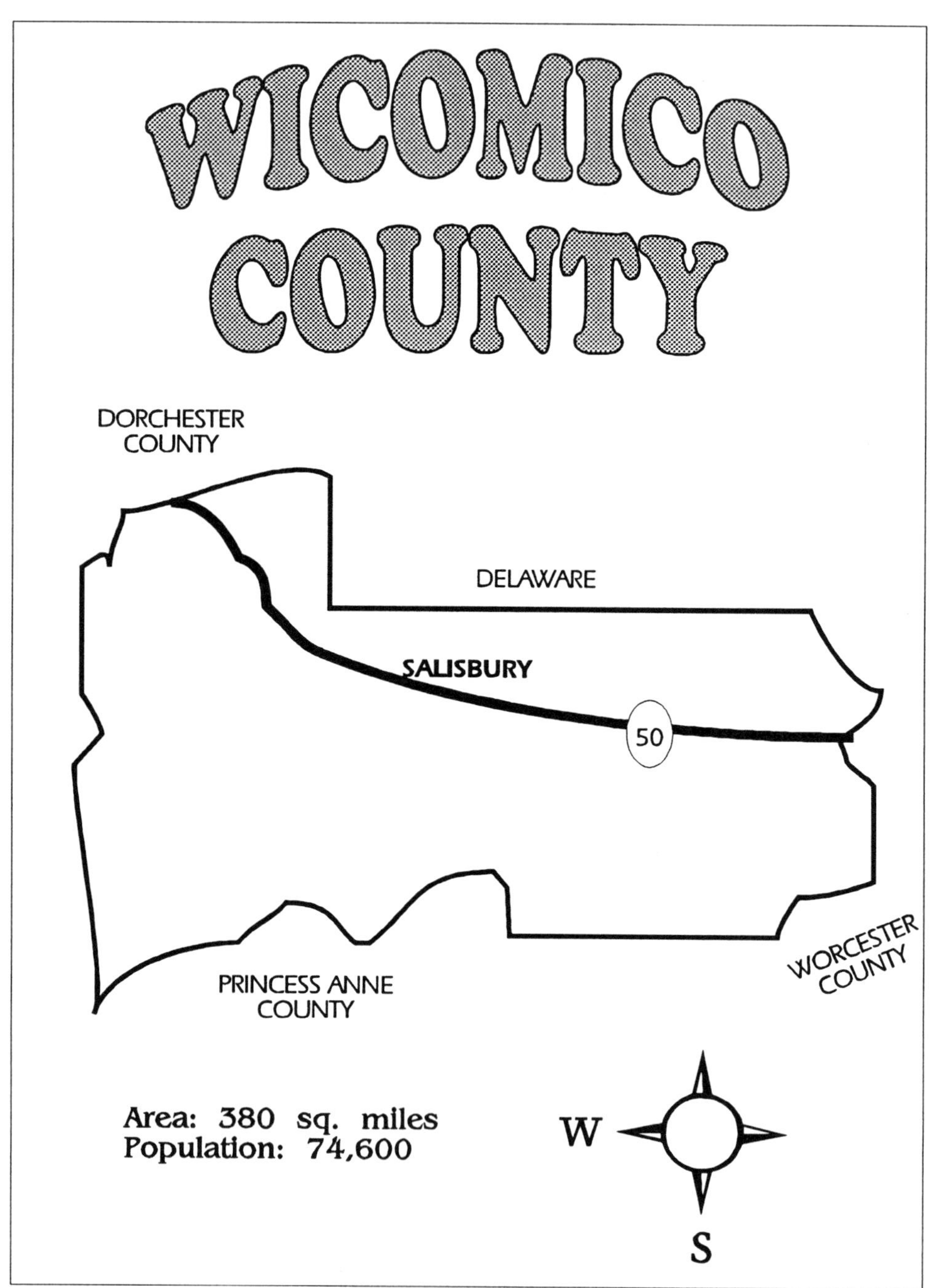
WICOMICO COUNTY
DORCHESTER COUNTY
DELAWARE
SALISBURY
50
PRINCESS ANNE COUNTY
WORCESTER COUNTY
Area: 380 sq. miles
Population: 74,600
W
S

JOHNNY & SAMMY'S

670 S. Salisbury Boulevard
Salisbury, MD
(410) 742-1116

YUPPIE APPEAL 2
MUNCH FACTOR 3
COMFORT ZONE 4
BUD QUOTIENT $1.75

Eighteen years ago, when I attended Salisbury State University, Johnny & Sammy's (est. 1946) was a legendary institution. While all of the other local watering holes were competing for the student and 29-and-under market, Johnny & Sammy was packing its house night after night with 40-and-over crowd - Salisbury's Old Money. It was there that I acquired an appreciation for the big band sounds of Dorsey, Goodman and Ellington.

A few years later, the restaurant/lounge had been sold, and the new owners gutted the lounge and put an all-you-can-eat crab bar in its place.

In the spring of 1992, the establishment again changed hands, and the first order of business by the new proprietors was to reinstate the lounge to its former status. The huge wildlife murals that graced the original enterprise were replaced. The room was filled with Salisbury's most comfortable lounge chairs, plus a huge, semi-circular sectional sofa was placed in front of the massive brick fireplace. And the original name, The Alpine Lounge, was reinstated.

Small trios playing the old tunes once again take the Alpine Lounge stage, and the favorite drinks (the martini and Manhattan) of the original enterprise are the favorites today.

Many of the patrons opt to get to the lounge early for dinner and a good seat for later in the evening. The complete restaurant menu is available in the lounge, and their half-pound burger served on a house-baked roll heads the list of lite fare. But if you visit Johnny & Sammy's Alpine Lounge from January through March, you'll have to try the specialty de la maison - muskrat.

For 30 years, the same chef has been preparing baked muskrat (heavily spiced with sage, slow cooked and served on a bed of hominy with turnip greens and cornbread on the side). It's Frank Perdue's, a regular Johnny & Sammy's patron, favorite. When the muskrat season is over, Frank orders the chicken.

Ever since the grand reopening, nearly all of the Alpine Lounge's patrons have made the same remark to their hostess; "We're so glad to have the place back."

BEST TIME TO VISIT

Chances for a good table are best on Wednesday and Thursday nights.

HOURS: Mon.-Fri. 11-1; Sat. 4-1; closed Sun.

HAPPY HOUR: Mon.-Fri. 4-7 half-priced drinks, hot munchies

ENTERTAINMENT: Wed. Sat. live oldies, MoR

ACCEPTABLE PLASTIC: V,MC

MARKET STREET INN

130 W. Market Street
Salisbury, MD
(301) 742-4145

YUPPIE APPEAL 4
MUNCH FACTOR 3
COMFORT ZONE 2
BUD QUOTIENT $2.10

The Market Street Inn is housed in a little two-story wood-planked house near the middle of the city. The place could use a coat or two of paint, and it looks like the next gale-force wind will reduce it to a pile of lumber. And yet, the Market Street Inn is the number one Yuppie destination in Salisbury. Oh, did I mention that the place is located on the water?

There are only a few commercial waterfront sites in Salisbury, and the Market Street Inn is the sole riverside food and drink establishment in town. The place may look a little rough on the outside, but the interior makes the Inn worth the trip. Its main room is filled with booths backed so high that they turn into mini private dining rooms. But the seats that patrons fight for are those surrounding the tables on the two porches perched directly on the Wicomico River.

Each of the tables, inside and out, contain the same articles: a shotglass filled with pencils, a jar of Grey Poupon, and a pad of menus. The Inn serves up good deli food with a twist. On one side of the menu is a list of 15 sandwiches from a $4.25 veggie pita to a $5.95 prime rib on a toasted roll. Each entry has a check box to be filled in by the customer. On the reverse side of the menu sheet, things get interesting. There are seven choices of bread, eight choices of meat, and six different cheeses. And for $4.95, customers can custom make their sandwich by checking off up to four meats and four cheeses. The same concept is used to create salads from 15 ingredients and 10 dressings.

Best selling spirits at the Market Street Inn are Absolut Vodka and Kahlua (as would be expected with such a yuppie-strong clientele), but a good 50 percent of drinks served there are the shooter variety, with the top creation being the "Baltimore Zoo," a $4 combination of vodka, gin, rum, triple sec, grenadine, sour mix and beer. The four major wine types of Sebastiani are available there by the glass.

During the spring and summer, the Market Street Inn is the leading cause of white collar absenteeism with businessmen leaving work early in hopes of snagging a riverside seat for Happy Hour.

HOURS: Mon.-Thurs. 11-1:30; Friday 11-2; Sat.-Sun. 1-8:30

HAPPY HOUR: Mon.-Fri. discount drafts, rail and wine

ENTERTAINMENT: Oldies via CD stereo

ACCEPTABLE PLASTIC: V,MC,AE

BEST TIME TO VISIT

Get there at three in the afternoon, and beat the businessmen.

MONTANA'S SPORTS BAR

810 Beaglin Park Drive
Salisbury, MD
(410) 543-4415

YUPPIE APPEAL 2
MUNCH FACTOR 4
COMFORT ZONE 4
BUD QUOTIENT $2.25

Montana's calls itself a sports pub, and with a continuous string of sporting events playing on seven large-screen TVs hooked up to three separate satellite dishes, I guess that's the correct category in which to place it. The bar side, which is totally separated from the restaurant side, is filled with sporting paraphernalia, posters and photos. But you don't have to be a sports lover to love Montana's Steakhouse & Sports Pub.

Beer lovers will love Montana's. Sticks at the bar announce the availability of only three domestic drafts, but if you look over the bar to the bottom of the backbar, you'll see a glass-faced refrigerator case (a la Fager's Island) filled with 40 imports and microbrews including Tsingtao, Swiss Lowenbrau, New Orleans' Dixie and Sam Smith's Oatmeal Stout (one of the best beers ever created). And if selection, Salisbury's best, isn't enough; on Tuesdays, all of those beers are sold for half price.

Shooter Lovers will love Montana's. During Thursday and Friday Happy Hours, Tooter (test tube) shooters cost 99 cents apiece, which is a pretty good deal. Bring a group of friends and buy an entire rack of Tooters for $19.99 (45 cents each).

Comedy Lovers will love Montana's. It's Salisbury's only comedy club featuring nationally prominent comedians once a month.

Carnivores will love Montana's. The entire steak house menu is available to pub patrons including steaks, ranging from a $9.95 top sirloin to a $39.95 32-ounce Angus porterhouse. There's even a certified Angus hot dog for $2.95.

Bargain hunters will love Montana's. For $7.95, the price of a half pound of spiced shrimp "down the ocean" (just 30 miles away), you can get a full pound of steamed shrimp and a pitcher of house brew (currently Coors Light) during Happy Hour. Or you can opt for four beef back ribs - two bucks. And it'll cost an extra 89 cents to wash them down with a mug of Coors. Get there between four and six p.m. and all menu entrees priced over $10.00 are discounted by five dollars.

BEST TIME TO VISIT

Personally, I think you should get there early on Tuesday to take advantage of the great listing of imported beers, all at half price.

HOURS: Mon.-Thurs. 11-1; Fri.-Sat. 11-2; Sun. 11-10

HAPPY HOUR: Mon.-Fri. 4-7 discount on various beers, liquors & shooters

ENTERTAINMENT: Monthly comedy shows

ACCEPTABLE PLASTIC: All

ROYAL EXCHANGE PUB

740 S. Salisbury Boulevard
Salisbury, MD
(301) 749-1263

YUPPIE APPEAL 4
MUNCH FACTOR 3
COMFORT ZONE 3
BUD QUOTIENT $1.75

Two decades ago, Salisbury was not the place to search for nighttime entertainment. That city just refused to compete with the resort 30 miles to the east. I remember as a student there, the best nightspot, other than those in Ocean City, was one in Seaford Delaware 15 miles away (and it wasn't much). How times have changed. If there had of been a Royal Exchange Pub in Salisbury during the early 70s, I would have saved a lot of money on gas.

The Royal Exchange is actually three separate and distinct operations: a full service restaurant, a tavern and a nightclub.

The backs of the booths in the pub are so high that they actually form 17 private alcoves, each comfortably sitting six. But before you take a seat there, check out the top of the bar. The drinking surface is a single five-inch thick slab of pine complete with bark and layered with about 50 coats of polyurethane. I've seen tables made like that, but never a bar. There's no real backbar. Instead, bar patrons face an exposed brick wall decorated with antique-framed mirrors and a bit of stained glass.

The liquor selection at the Royal Exchange is slightly better than most of its contemporaries. Along with a full complement of imported vodkas are quite a few super-premium offerings including The Macallan and Glenmorangie single malts.

There are 15 beers to choose (mostly domestics) and Sutter Home varieties in the small bottles (187ml) to go with an admirable selection of pub food featuring over a dozen finger foods and 15 sandwiches.

Pass through a couple of doors and you're in the Liverpool Flying Club, the Royal Exchange's nightclub, where rock and top-40 music is spun by a DJ during the latter half of the week, and jazz is played live by "Shore Jazz" on the second or third Sunday of the month.

The Liverpool Flying Club is also the site of numerous promotions such as bikini contests, lambada contest, and a contest which the management asked me not to mention because of some flack they received from a local group of blue noses.

HOURS: Mon.-Sat. 11-2; Sun. 12-10

HAPPY HOUR: Mon.-Fri. 4-7 all drinks but premiums are half-price

ENTERTAINMENT: Wed.-Sat. DJ rock

ACCEPTABLE PLASTIC: V, MC, AE, D

BEST TIME TO VISIT

The place is at its peak on Fridays. Get to the pub before seven, or to the nightclub before nine.

WEBSTER'S 1801

1801 N. Salisbury Boulevard
Salisbury, MD
(410) 742-8000

YUPPIE APPEAL 2
MUNCH FACTOR 4
COMFORT ZONE 4
BUD QUOTIENT $2.25

In this era of raised consciousness, increased sensitivity, *Steel Magnolias*, and Phil Donahue, it's nice to know that the classic "Meat Market" hasn't disappeared from the Maryland nightlife scene. Just walk into Webster's 1801 on any Friday night.

Webster's is the biggest, boldest and brassiest nightclub in Salisbury and, on Friday, crowds nearing the four-digit mark crush their way into the place for "Pretty Woman" night where females pay five dollars at the door for all the beer, wine and spirits they can hold. Guys have to pay full price on Friday nights but, for some reason, they don't seem to mind. And the normally sedate club at the north end of town rocks (literally) until two.

Other evenings during the week at Webster's are slightly more sane. Movies play on the megabuck Mitsubishi 35-inch monitor (one of the few you'll ever see in a bar) on Mondays. Four doctors from Seaford, Delaware, calling themselves the "Medics Quintet," perform easy-listening jazz on Wednesdays there. And every Thursday, Webster's cooks up a whole pig and gives it away during the weekly Luau Night.

On Saturdays, the "Pretty Woman" promotion is repeated but the patrons mostly enter the doors two by two, unlike the Friday version where it's every man and woman for himself/herself.

Webster's 1801 is one of the newer kids on the block, opening May 1990, but it has already achieved a lock on the Friday night college-age crowd. It's main lounge is a huge, high room filled with booths and extremely comfortable chairs, with the large square bar serving as the centerpiece. To accommodate the horde descending on the place on "Pretty Woman" night, two adjacent lounges, each with their own full bar, are opened.

Only a handful of beers are available from the bar, and the wine selection is small. But over 100 different shooters (many being house creations) are available, and have become the drinks of choice among the Webster's patrons.

Best bets on food there (served until one) have crab as the major ingredient: dips, cakes and stuffed mushrooms.

BEST TIME TO VISIT

Friday night (singles), Thursday nights (couples).

HOURS: Mon.-Sat. 11-2; Sun. 11-10

HAPPY HOUR: Mon.-Fri. 4-7 all drinks and hot foods half-price

ENTERTAINMENT: Tues.-Sat. DJ rock

ACCEPTABLE PLASTIC: All but CB

WORCESTER COUNTY

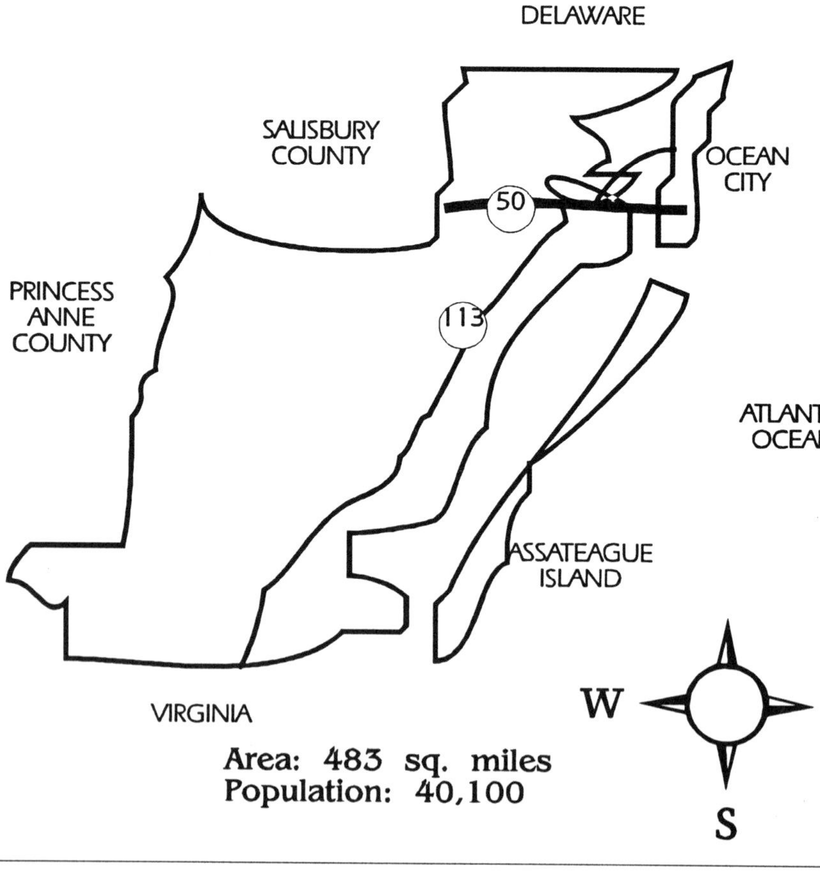

DELAWARE

SALISBURY COUNTY

OCEAN CITY

50

PRINCESS ANNE COUNTY

113

ATLANTIC OCEAN

ASSATEAGUE ISLAND

VIRGINIA

W

S

Area: 483 sq. miles
Population: 40,100

B.J.'S ON THE WATER

75th Street & the Bay
Ocean City, MD
(410) 524-7575

YUPPIE APPEAL 3
MUNCH FACTOR 4
COMFORT ZONE 4
BUD QUOTIENT $2.10

And the award for the best sit-down bar on the bay goes to...B.J.'s on the Water (thunderous applause). Of course, the place doesn't just rest on the laurels bestowed on its great bar - but it could. It's thc kind of bar you'd find in Georgetown or Annapolis; if you were lucky. The big and beautiful mahogany bar adorned above with stained glass panels sets atop a hardwood floor, and below a set of antique fans slowly rotating beneath an ornate stamped tin ceiling. This is not your ordinary beach bar.

As you continue to scan the interior of B.J.'s, the scene shifts from the 1920's to the 1990's. Ten video monitors coupled to two rooftop satellite dishes are scattered about the two major rooms comprising the place's eating and drinking area. If there's a sporting event on the tube anywhere, it'll be on display there.

Have at least one drink at B.J.'s wonderful old bar before strolling to the adjacent raw bar (Ocean City's largest) surrounded by windows overlooking the bay. There, an S-shaped bar, seating 20, was designed solely for those who crave the uncooked or steamed stuff.

Fifteen beers (all of the familiar bottled offerings) plus three domestics drafts are served at the bar. The wines of Inglenook and Los Hermanos make up the house wines by the glass, and the spirits selection should satisfy all. Nearly a dozen frozen drinks made with either ice or ice cream are house specialties, with the most special specialty being their Razzamatazz raspberry colada.

Do you think you can eat 50 steamed clams or steamed oysters at one sitting? Here's the place to find out. A bucket of fifty of those shellfish costs $25.

Of course, I guess you could always bring someone with you to share that voluminous appetizer.

Not only does B.J.'s serve up nearly 20 different sandwiches, and a dozen other varieties of great finger foods, they do it later than anyone else. When other waterfront kitchens have closed for the night, B.J.'s cooks keep at it until 1:30 in the a.m.

Oh, do you like ducks? B.J.'s has adopted about 100, and the 1 a.m. daily duck feeding has become a bayside event.

BEST TIME TO VISIT

Make sure you've secured a good seat for the daily setting of the sun.

HOURS: Mon.-Sun. 11-2

HAPPY HOUR: Mon.-Fri. 4-7 discount drinks and steamed shrimp

ENTERTAINMENT: Mon. & Wed. live rock; scheduled deck parties in summer

ACCEPTABLE PLASTIC: All but D

COINS PUB

28th Street & Coastal Highway
Ocean City, MD
(410) 289-3100

YUPPIE APPEAL 1
MUNCH FACTOR 3
COMFORT ZONE 3
BUD QUOTIENT $1.75

There once was a man named Coyne who worked for 35 years a president of an auto supply company in Baltimore. And one day, he bought something he always wanted - an Ocean City bar. It wasn't a bar with a great reputation, and it wasn't a big bar (by Ocean City standards), but it was his bar and that was enough.

After scouting out the local market, Coyne decided to operate a locals' bar, a bar like the bars he frequented in East Baltimore. And so, he did.

Coins is a very comfortable and friendly little watering hole located at the north end of a small strip shopping center. Once inside, you'll see none of the expected resort trappings. The walls display framed landscapes and wildlife paintings. And the big oval bar is ringed with cozy booths and tables.

Even in the midst of the tourists season, at least half of the Coins' patrons will be locals, and during the off-season, the place becomes one of the most popular watering holes for those who live and work in and around the island. Why has the place become so popular with those who call Ocean City their home town? Price.

One of the major factors Coyne had to consider before opting to open a Ocean City pub for locals was the locals' level of disposable cash - which ain't high. So to entice the regional populace, there's $1.25 rail drinks and beer every afternoon, five house wines going for $2 a glass, and an unbelievable luncheon deal. The daily lunch special (e.g. a platterful of meatloaf, mashed potatoes and green beans) goes for $1.39 (no, that's not a misprint).

Five drafts including Moosehead are for sale along with a dozen bottled brands. And the backbar spirit selection is fairly complete.

It's an older crowd that frequents Coins, and live entertainment (mostly playing the tunes of the 50s and 60s) is served up every night during the summer.

Sure, you may be able to get the same food & beverage deals and entertainment offered by Coins at home in your neighborhood bar. But when your funds are running low at the beach, it's nice to know they're there.

HOURS: Mon.-Sun. 11-2

HAPPY HOUR: Mon.-Fri. 3-6 domestic beer & rail drinks for $1.25

ENTERTAINMENT: Nightly live oldies bands in summer; weekends in winter

ACCEPTABLE PLASTIC: V, MC

BEST TIME TO VISIT

Anytime you want to escape from the general mayhem of Ocean City.

FAGER'S ISLAND

60th Street in the Bay
Ocean City, MD
(410) 524-5500

YUPPIE APPEAL 5
MUNCH FACTOR 5
COMFORT ZONE 3
BUD QUOTIENT $2.50

I could go on and on about the location of Fager's Island, and the magnificent view it affords it's patrons. But the address alone tells the story (60th Street **IN** the Bay), and to make sure customers are looking in the right direction at the right time, sunsets are signaled daily in the island retreat by a stirring rendition of Tchaikovsky's *1812 Overture* (you know, the old Quaker Puffed Rice theme song).

Enough about things scenic. Let's go into things gastronomic. No other tavern in Ocean City offers its patrons a selection of food and drink like Fager's Island, period.

You're on vacation. You're "down the ocean." Make the most of it. Belly up to the bar, but don't order right away. Pick up the menus.

Ninety-nine different brews are listed on the beer menu. Your favorites are all there, but so are a bunch of exotics and super exotics: Orval Trappist Ale from Belgium, Brasseurs from France, MacAndrews from Scotland (although the menu says its from England). If you're a Bud drinker, try an Indian Kingfisher or a New Zealand Steinlager. Mich Dry buffs should try an Aashi Super Dry from Japan. And for something completely different, sip a sweet & fruity Belgian Framboise. On tap, there's one beer that you can't get anywhere but Fager's - Blue Dog - brewed exclusively for the establishment by the Wild Goose Brewery in nearby Cambridge.

Wine drinkers at Fager's Island are in for an even biggest treat. At the bar, 12 premium wines are offered by the glass, and over 400 **(FOUR HUNDRED)** labels are available in full bottles or splits (half bottles).

And at the hot and cold ends of the potent potable spectrum, Fager's offers the choice of 13 "Island Coffees," and nine different tall and frozen concoctions.

OK. You've chosen your beverage. Now it's time to order a bit of pub grub: smoked salmon, baked brie, stuffed mushrooms, rumacki, half-pound burgers, coconut shrimp, the list goes on and on.

Bon Apetit.

BEST TIME TO VISIT

Get there about a half hour before sunset during the less crowded weekdays, and settle in for the evening.

HOURS: Mon.-Sun. 11-2

HAPPY HOUR: Mon.-Fri. 4-7 discount drinks

ENTERTAINMENT: Wed.-Sun live bands (summer); Fri.-Sat. (winter)

ACCEPTABLE PLASTIC: V, MC, AE, DC

OCEAN CLUB

49th Street & Coastal Highway
Ocean City, MD
(410) 524-7500

YUPPIE APPEAL	4
MUNCH FACTOR	4
COMFORT ZONE	4
BUD QUOTIENT	$2.10

As nice as the premier Ocean City bayside clubs are, there's this one little thing that they just don't have - the Atlantic. Yes, the bayside spots have got a lock on all those beautiful sunsets, but when you go "down the ocean," don't you really want to see the ocean? If so, one of the very best vantage spots is the Ocean Club, inside or out.

If you've been reading this guide from front to back, you've already discovered that I give a lot of credit to bars with ornate or imaginative backbars; they're an integral part of the bargoing experience. There's no backbar at the Ocean Club bar. Instead bar patrons there have a great view of the ocean and beach.

HOURS: Mon.-Sun. 11:30-2

HAPPY HOUR: Mon.-Fri. 4-7 discount drinks

ENTERTAINMENT: Mon.-Sun. live top-40 bands

ACCEPTABLE PLASTIC: V, MC, AE, DC

Bravo! Most, but not all, beachfront resort food & beverage operations insist on giving their dining patrons all of the choice windowfront property, but the interior of the octagonal Ocean Club is so spacious (it can comfortably hold 175) and well laid-out that almost everyone (except in packed house situations) gets their own personal oceanview, even those perched at the bar.

During the summer, that Ocean Club's oceanview gets even better as the daytime action transfers to the huge 125-seat outdoor bar and patio ringed with 30 to 40 live palm trees. As an added incentive for making the trip to the Ocean Club's outdoor facility (as if you needed one), there's a steel band performing every summer weekend.

Fifteen beers (including Sam Adams, Red Stripe and Grolsch) and three domestic draft offerings can be had inside or outside at the Club, and the house wines (Sebastiani) are accompanied by a featured special wine which changes daily.

Munchies there are as quality-laden as the view: fresh lump crab cake, overstuffed sandwiches of roast beef, smoked turkey or peppered Italian ham, and grilled mahimahi with the works on a kaiser to name a few. And if you visit the Ocean Club in the off-season, the palm trees outside may be sagging a bit, but the Lite Fare menu is offered at half price every afternoon.

Every night of the week, there's live top-40 happening on stage, with plenty of room beneath a sea of Casablanca fans to dance or just relax.

BEST TIME TO VISIT

Friday Happy Hours at the Ocean Club are an event.

O.C. SEACRETS

117 W. 49th Street
Ocean City, MD
(410) 524-4900

YUPPIE APPEAL 4
MUNCH FACTOR 5
COMFORT ZONE 5
BUD QUOTIENT $2.25

I hardly know where to begin. This place is like no other in Ocean City, or the entire state for that matter. O.C. Seacrets is not your stereotypical resort club; it's more of a state of mind.

Each April, 700 tropical plants and trees (40 varieties in all including bird of paradise, palms and bougainvillaea) are planted in this 30,000 square foot complex, transforming the O.C. bayfront site into a tropical paradise. After one Rum Runner, you'll think you died and went to Jamaica (after three rum runners, you'll just die).

Food and drink can be enjoyed there in four distinct location: an all-season bar/lounge/greenhouse, an open-air thatched hut, a winding bayside patio, or on a personal raft in the bay.

Although the beer and spirit selection rivals the other bayfront establishments, except for Fager's Island (featured herein), the drinks to drink at Seacrets are the ones as unique as the place itself. Throughout the complex, there are eight converted frozen custard machines dispensing either a mild, creamy pina colada or a plenty potent rum runner (three of which could debilitate most breeds of livestock). Although both frozen concoctions are delicious as they are, the ultimate bayside drink is the Pain in de Ass, a layered mixture of the two. Vodka & tonic drinkers should opt for Some Ting & Vodka - a much more refreshing highball. Since the place doesn't profess to create the world's greatest Bloody Mary, they instead set up a Bloody Mary bar to let patrons create their own.

The above rule for choosing drinks at Seacrets also applies to the munchies: go with the grub that's solely

available there such as the Jammin' burger (watch out, it's deceptively hot), fresh dough Jamaican pizza, and the best finger food at the beach (my opinion, of course), Jerk Chicken - chunks of chicken breast marinated for a day or two in a wonderful melange of spices, then quickly broiled and served with honey mustard. In their first year, Seacrets sold nine tons of that awesome appetizer.

BEST TIME TO VISIT

Between September 15 and October 15, or April 15 and May 15, you can stretch ot there and forget and your cares. The place is jammed in the summer.

HOURS: Mon.-Sun. 11-2

HAPPY HOUR: Mon.-Fri. 4-7 discount drinks (summer); Mon.-Sun 4-7 (winter)

ENTERTAINMENT: Sun. live bands; Tues. deck parties

ACCEPTABLE PLASTIC: V, MC, AE

PURPLE MOOSE

108 S. Boardwalk
Ocean City, MD
(410) 289-6953

YUPPIE APPEAL 4
MUNCH FACTOR 0
COMFORT ZONE 2
BUD QUOTIENT $2.50

How do you remember the Purple Moose? As a randy college hangout? As a down and out biker bar? Those were some of the stages that the place went through. But in 1987, the tavern was expanded to more than double its original size and took on a new persona, the one it carries today - a friendly neighborhood tavern (that happens to be situated atop Maryland's most valuable real estate).

From the outside, the Moose still appears to be the narrow Boardwark liquor parlor it was a decade ago. But walk through the door today and you'll see one of Ocean City's biggest sit-down bars (maybe the biggest) capable of serving nearly 100 patrons at a time. The saloon, itself, doesn't fill to capacity until it reaches the 300-customer mark.

The Purple Moose Bloody Mary, purported to be the World's Best (you be the judge), arrives complete with celery stick and cucumber slice. Their equally highly touted frozen pina colada is made with all fresh ingredients and it's created using no crushed ice.

Beers at the Moose are the standard variety with no draft offerings, but they do have an admiral selection of liquors and liqueurs. And during those frigid seaside nights, the place is a true haven from the cold. Forty different International spiked coffees, from Dutch (with Vandermint) to South American (banana liqueur), are served at the bar.

Forget about eating there. The Moose has no intention of competing with the hundreds of Boardwalk vendors.

Live bands play rock & roll at the Moose weekends during the spring and fall, and nightly during the summer. Plans are being made to have a DJ on hand before the musicians take the stage this summer.

Along with the expansion of floor space at the Purple Moose came an expansion in the "Moose Collection." Still Ocean City's number one bar t-shirt, the traditional purple Purple Moose shirt has been joined by about 25 other shirts (size: infant to XXX) bearing the bar's logo and a host of other wearables such as jockey shorts and panties, a $1.98 set of Moose antlers and a $44.95 Purple Moose satin jacket.

HOURS: Mon.-Sun. 11:30-2

HAPPY HOUR: Mon.-Sat. 10-2; Sun. 12:30-2

ENTERTAINMENT: Nightly live bands (summer); Fri.-Sat. live (off-season)

ACCEPTABLE PLASTIC: V, MC, AE, DC

BEST TIME TO VISIT

Between 2-6, you'll meet the best mix of people at the Moose.

INDEX TO ESTABLISHMENTS

A.L. GATOR'S 8
ALONSO'S 18
ANDY'S 87
B.J.'S ON THE WATER 115
BALLS 19
BALTIMORE BREWING CO. 20
BANDALOOPS 21
BOWIE INN 94
BRAVO 59
BROWN PELICAN 65
BUDDIES 22
CACAO LANE 81
CADILLAC JACK'S 103
CAFE TATTOO 23
CAT'S EYE PUB 24
COINS 116
CORNER BAR 25
COUNTRY DOCKS 48
P.J. CRICKETT'S 26

DANIEL'S 82
DEAD EYE SALOON 27
DOCKSIDE 54
DONNELLY'S 66
DRIFTWOOD INN 44
FAGER'S ISLAND 117
GEORGETOWN NORTH 77
GLADSTONE'S 2
GRIFFIN'S 9
HANGAR CLUB 95
HANCOCK TAVERN 106
HARBOR HOUSE 55
HAWTHORNE'S 96
HENNY'S 3
HIGHTOPPS 28
HONI-HONI 72
HUBCAP INN 29
HULL STREET BLUES 30
HUMMERS 78

ISLAND INN 60
J.B.'S STEAK CELLAR 4
JENNIFER'S 67
JOHNNY & SAMMY'S 109
KANGAROO KATIE'S 97
KISLING'S 31
KITTY KNIGHT HOUSE 88
LAST CHANCE SALOON 83
LA TRATTORIA 68
MACGREGOR'S 79
MALARKEY'S 90
MARKET STREET CAFE 56
MARKET STREET INN 110
McCAULEY'S PUB 61
McDONALD'S RAW BAR 69
McGARVEY'S SALOON 10
MIDDLETON TAVERN 11
MILTON INN 45
MONTANA'S SPORTS BAR 111
NANTUCKET LANDING 91
NAUGHTY GULL 49
NOKLEBY'S 104
OASIS NITE CLUB 32
OCEAN CLUB 118
OLIVER'S 98
O'TOOLE'S 99
OWL BAR 33

PECORA BAYSIDE 12
PERRY INN & PUB 46
PHOENIX EMPORIUM 84
PIRATE'S COVE 13
PURPLE MOOSE 120
RAM'S HEAD TAVERN 14
RED EYE'S DOCK BAR 101
RIVERBOAT 62
ROBERTSON'S CRAB HOUSE 63
ROYAL EXCHANGE PUB 112
ROY'S PLACE 92
RUSTY SCUPPER 34

SCAMPY'S II 5
SCARLETT COVE CAFE 35
SCHAEFER'S CANAL HOUSE 57
O.C. SEACRETS 119
SHENANIGANS 73
SILVER TREE 74
SISSON'S 36
SNEAKERS 85
SOLOMONS PIER 50
STRAY CAT CAFE 75
TELL TALE HEARTH 37
TIKI BAR 51
TIMBUKTU 15
TIO LOCO'S 38
TOPSIDE INN 16
VERA'S WHITE SANDS 52
WAG'S 70
WATERFRONT HOTEL 39
WAYSIDE INN 107
WEBER'S ON BOSTON 40
WEBSTER'S 1801 113
WHISTLE STOP 41
WINE CELLAR 6
YOUNG BIN 42

BEST TIME TO VISIT

(A=afternnon E=evening N=night F=fall S=summer W=winter)

A.L. Gator's (N)
Alonso's (E)
Andy's (N)
B.J.'s on the Water (E,S)
Balls (E)
Baltimore Brewing Co. (E)
Bandaloops (E,W)
Bowie Inn (E)
Bravo (E)
Brown Pelican (N)
Buddies (N)

Cacao Lane (E)
Cadillac Jack's (N)
Cafe Tattoo (E)
Cat's Eye Pub (N)
Coins (E,S)
Corner Bar (E)
Country Docks (N)
P.J. Crickett's (E)
Daniel's (A,S)
Dead Eye Saloon (E,S)
Dockside (A,S)
Donnelly's (E)
Driftwood Inn (E,S)

Fager's Island (E,S)
Georgetown North (E)
Gladstone's (E,W)
Griffin's (E)
Hangar Club (N)
Hancock Tavern (A)
Harbor House (A, S)
Hawthorne's (E)
Henny's (E)
Hightopps (A, S)

Honi-Honi (E,S)
Hubcap Inn (E)
Hull Street Blues (E)
Hummers (N)
Island Inn (A,S)
J.B.'s Steak Cellar (E)
Jennifer's (E,W)
Johnny & Sammy's (E,W)
Kangaroo Katie's (N)
Kisling's (E)
Kitty Knight House (E,W)

Last Chance Saloon (E)
La Trattoria (E)
MacGregor's (E)
Malarkey's (E)
Market Street Cafe (E)
Market Street Inn (A,S)
McCauley's Pub (E)
McDonald's Raw Bar (N)
McGarvey's Saloon (E)
Middleton Tavern (E)
Milton Inn (A,W)

Montana's Sports Bar (E)
Nantucket Landing (E)
Naughty Gull (E,S)
Nokleby's (N)
Oasis Nite Club (N)
Ocean Club (E,S)
Oliver's (E)
O'Toole's (E)
Owl Bar (E)
Pecora Bayside (A,S)
Perry Inn & Pub (E)
Phoenix Emporium (E)

Pirate's Cove (E,S)
Purple Moose (E,S)
Ram's Head Tavern (E)
Red Eye's Dock Bar (A,S)
Riverboat (E,S)
Robertson's Crab House (A,S)
Royal Exchange Pub (E)
Roy's Place (E)
Rusty Scupper (A)
Scampy's II (E,S)

Scarlett Cove Cafe (E)
Schaefer's Canal House (A,S)
O.C. Seacrets (E,F)
Shenanigans (E,W)
Silver Tree (E,S)
Sisson's (E)
Sneakers (E)
Solomons Pier (E,S)
Stray Cat Cafe (E)
Tell Tale Hearth (E)
Tiki Bar (A,S)
Timbuktu (E)

Tio Loco's (E)
Topside Inn (E)
Vera's White Sands (A,S)
Wag's (E)
Waterfront Hotel (E)
Wayside Inn (N)
Weber's on Boston (E)
Webster's 1801 (N)
Whistle Stop (E)
Wine Cellar (E)
Young Bin (N)

SPECIALTIES OF THE HOUSE

Although most establishments in this guide have well-rounded food and beverage menus, some operations have become well-known for a single offering such as the places listed below:

Alonso's (burgers)
Balt. Brewing Co. (beer)
Bravo (pizza)
Cafe Tattoo (barbecue)
Coins (crab cake)
Corner Bar (spirits)

J.B.'s Steak Cellar (beef)
Last Chance Saloon (draft beer)
La Trattoria (pizza)
Purple Moose (Bloody Mary)
Robertson's (crabs)
Roy's Place (sandwiches)

Sisson's (beer)
Tell Tale Hearth (pizza)
Tiki Bar (mai tai)
Tio Loco's (tequila)
Vera's (South Sea's drinks)
Young Bin (dried squid)

THE GREAT OUTDOORS

The following establishments offer al fresco drinking & dining either seasonally or year-round:

B.J.'s on the Water
Balls
Cacao Lane
Cafe Tattoo
Country Docks
P.J. Crickett's
Daniel's
Dead Eye Saloon
Dockside
Driftwood Inn
Fager's Island
Harbor House
Henny's
Hightopps
Honi-Honi
Hubcap Inn
Kitty Knight House
La Trattoria
MacGregor's
Malarkey's
Market Street Cafe
Market Street Inn
McDonald's Raw Bar *
Middleton Tavern
Milton Inn
Ocean Club
Oliver's
Pecora Bayside
Pirate's Cove
Ram's Head Tavern
Red Eye's Dock Bar
Riverboat
Rusty Scupper
Scampy's II
Schaefer's Canal House
O.C. Seacrets
Silver Tree
Solomons Pier
Tiki Bar
Vera's White Sands

(* Coming next year)

THE GUIDE TO TAVERNS, CLUBS & BARS
is a great gift idea

Fill in and mail today while supplies last

Paperback, autographed, first edition - $8.95
please add $2.00 shipping per book

A gift card will be enclosed with each book

Make out check and mail to:
Journal Books
7451 Race Road
P.O. Box 1002
Hanover, MD 21076
Phone: (410) 796-5455
FAX: (410) 796-5511

PLEASE CUT ALONG DOTTED LINE

PLEASE TYPE OR PRINT CLEARLY

Please send a copy of THE GUIDE TO MARYLAND TAVERNS, CLUBS & BARS to:

NAME ______________________

ADDRESS ______________________

CITY, STATE & ZIP ______________________

gift card message ______________________

FROM:
NAME ______________________

ADDRESS ______________________

CITY, STATE & ZIP ______________________

Check/Money Order Enclosed $ __________

SIGNATURE ______________________

Please send a copy of THE GUIDE TO MARYLAND TAVERNS, CLUBS & BARS to:

NAME ______________________

ADDRESS ______________________

CITY, STATE & ZIP ______________________

gift card message ______________________

FROM:
NAME ______________________

ADDRESS ______________________

CITY, STATE & ZIP ______________________

Check/Money Order Enclosed $ __________

SIGNATURE ______________________